AF324306

24 / 7

Stories of Faith
From Everyday Life

Bruce Boyer

December 2015

24 / 7

Stories of Faith
From Everyday Life

Bruce Boyer

Published by
Alabaster Book Publishing
North Carolina

Published by Alabaster Book Publishing
P.O. Box 401
Kernersville, North Carolina 27285
www.PublisherAlabaster.biz

Book design by
D.L.Shaffer

Cover photo by
Gene Stafford, Gene Stafford Photography

First Edition

ISBN: 978-0-9912660-6-7

Library of Congress Control Number
2014921888

This book is dedicated to The Old Gray Goose,
mentor and role model, who taught me the importance
of Christian leadership and sharing my faith.

Acknowledgements

The most important acknowledgement in any devotional book
is the inspiration of the Holy Spirit. God constantly makes me
aware of storylines that provide faith lesson ideas. My chief reference guide is the <u>Holy Bible</u>. For a story to be Godly, it must
back up faith lessons with scriptural references. These stories are
about God at work, not humans. *For it is by grace you have been saved,
through faith – and this not from yourselves, it is the gift of God – not by
works, so that no one can boast. For we are God's workmanship, created in
Christ Jesus to do good works, which God prepared in advance for us to do
(Ephesians 2:8-10).*

I have been fortunate for a lifetime of employment at the YMCA
and Chamber of Commerce, allowing the opportunity to present devotional thoughts on a regular basis. Being a camper and
counselor at YMCA resident Camp Kenan emphasized the three
equal sides of the YMCA triangle: Spirit, Mind and Body. As
a teenager I presented daily devotions and "morning thoughts"
at YMCA camp. While some devotions came out of devotional
books, I began developing my own story ideas, showing God at
work in a way children could understand.

I am dedicating this book to The Old Gray Goose from YMCA
Camp Kenan, my mentor during the formative young adult
years of my life. The Old Gray Goose was a tireless servant and
wonderful Christian role model. For Goose, being a YMCA
professional was a "calling." I chose a career in the YMCA as my
calling, largely because of his example.

The devotions in this book are my own ideas from things I
see in the community. Terra Lynn Dearth, National Director
for YMCA Christian Leadership Conferences/Rags & Leath-
ers program, has been a big influence helping me connect the
dots between spiritual knowledge and practical application. The
purpose of YMCA Christian Leadership Conferences is to train
YMCA staff to teach and model Christian values through YMCA

programs. Few people realize the first YMCA (1844) was a Bible study organization. Even though today's YMCA is more comprehensive, I consider it an opportunity for personal ministry.

Once I put devotional ideas to paper I often consult with friends to see if the faith lesson is clearly stated. I would like to thank Bob Kahle, a YMCA camp director who is the best contemporary Christian storyteller I have ever met. Russ Tedder has a creative mind who can find God-sightings and unique ways of articulating events from a Christian perspective. I often sent the stories to Bob and Russ for their opinion and guidance.

My pastor at Fountain of Life Lutheran Church, Dr. Rick Meyer, guided me on the format to include a thought-provoking question and closing prayer to each story. The question helped transform the writings from a feel-good story to having a personal application.

My wife, Kathy Boyer, provided the reality check, screening of stories, and initial grammatical review. She also allowed me time to work on the stories at the expense of other "honey-do" projects I could have been doing. Family friend and Kernersville Middle School Language Arts teacher, Jeff Shu, and his wife, Lisa, provided the final editing for the stories.

The cover photo of this book is courtesy of Gene Stafford, of Gene Stafford Photography. The cover photo is of the signature stained glass sanctuary windows of my church, Fountain of Life Lutheran Church.

These stories are just a starting point. My hope is the stories will enhance your awareness of God at work all around you, and acknowledge Jesus Christ as your Lord and Savior.

Table of Contents

Stories

Title	Topic	Page

Introduction

It is Sunday morning. Families rush off to church to worship. Check. Stay for Sunday school. Hopefully, check. Stop at a restaurant for lunch on the way home. Check. Now that the "obligations" are checked off we have the rest of the week for everything else on our crowded to-do list. No check mark here. Being a person of faith is not a one or two-hour-a-week obligation. God doesn't want to be just a mark on your checklist. He wants to be part of your life 24/7 -- all of it.

While the pastor may unpack a scriptural passage in the sermon and be supported by an appropriate choral anthem, there is more to understanding God's impact on your life than what you take away from the weekly church service. God's impact is how you live your life all 168 hours a week. He wants to see how you apply His Word and Sabbath message throughout the entire week. God doesn't limit Himself to the day of worship.

The purpose of this book is to show examples of how God works in our lives 24/7. He is there in our relationships with people, and in all the events of our lives. When we don't constrain God's influence on our behavior to one day of the week we open our hearts to seek Him in everything we do.

Though the humble efforts of these stories never will replace time God wants you to spend reading his Word and in public worship, they can be used for personal devotion or for inspirational messages at the beginning of meetings. On the surface, the stories provide a motivational message to help people see a purpose to their efforts. In the deeper sense, it shows God's influence on our everyday lives. Many groups, such as YMCAs, also intentionally use devotions in child care, summer camp and even sports settings. Organizations with a Christian purpose will find these stories and their accompanying faith lessons helpful at the beginning of their meetings. But there is more. The stories include a personal question to ponder, scriptural reference, and a concluding prayer. For consistency, scriptural references are of the NIV translation.

Though not intended as an in-depth Bible study, each story contains a scriptural verse illustrating a key point from the story. The scriptural reference ensures faith lessons are in line with God and not our own theology. Additional scripture references are also included at the end of this book. The stories are light enough to be of interest to anyone, but inspirational to people of faith. Our role as a follower of Jesus Christ is relatively simple: plant the seeds and let the Holy Spirit do the rest. Yes, the overall purpose of this book is to encourage people in their faith, but without a baseball bat to drive the point home, or worse yet, drive people away. Stories catch people's interest and allow others to hear the message at their own level of understanding. The faith lesson helps people associate a biblical reference with the everyday story. It is how Jesus taught. He told stories. There is not, nor will there ever be, a better example to follow. Come, and follow the Master.

Feature Story Part I: Lost in the Amazon
Why Am I So Committed?

Is This The Tragic End?

It wasn't the usual late Friday afternoon call from my wife. Typically, Kathy would call to have me pick up a pizza or stop at the store for milk on the way home from work. Today was different. I could tell the moment she started speaking. Kathy was calling me home because she had just received a phone call from the U.S. Embassy in Brazil. Our son, Dave, and a friend had been reported missing in the Amazon rainforest. Exploring the pristine natural environment had been their dream, but now had become a nightmare for all of us. When we were contacted, they had already been missing for four days in the densest rainforest in the world. They were without food and water. At the time, we didn't know what the future held for any of us. That telephone call and the succeeding events would change our lives forever.

Dave Boyer in Amazon rain forest

Their journey was anything but a casual stroll in the park. The

Bruce Boyer

Amazon rainforest is a breathtaking panoramic scene of timeless nature. Every square inch is alive with a combination of insects, birds, venomous snakes, monkeys, and other jungle wildlife. Thick vegetation constantly attempts to reclaim the land, creating an unmerciful struggle for survival for everything in the rainforest. People are the intruders in this beautiful but hostile environment. Its moist, humid climate hosts the largest number of plant species on Earth. Located close to the equator, night and day are equally divided, with nightfall placing our missing hikers in total darkness.

Communication was difficult with that undeveloped part of the world. A cell phone conversation with the owner of the remote youth hostel where they were staying informed us all tracks of the hikers had been washed away in a severe rainstorm. The last footsteps found showed them headed deeper into the jungle. In the days that followed, daily communications with the US Embassy in Brasilia gave us reassurances of search efforts, but stopped well short of any promise of survival. We had hope, but that came from our faith in God, not from any sense of realism. There were times we, as parents, began to calculate the odds of survival. We quickly had to turn our thoughts to God and his power or the realism of the situation would overtake us. The question of whether they were dead or alive weighed heavily. As parents, we took comfort in the hope God had a plan, and made that our anchor. Thankfully, six members of our church spent the entire Saturday with us, bolstering our hopes.

There was little we could do, except pray. On day six, thousands of miles away, our son and his companion had reached a breaking point. Their only chance for survival was finding a river that might lead to civilization. Manmade trails were virtually non-existent, only present near civilized areas along rivers. They had a major force working against them. Before their hike started, the owner of the hostel created a crude, hand-drawn sketch of the area. But she oriented the drawing in the opposite direction as expected,

Stories of Faith from Everyday Life

with north at the bottom of the map. Using it for navigation was a formula for disaster, taking them deeper into the rainforest. The map was their anchor in their attempts to find their way out but it was 180 degrees incorrect. In the days that followed, hundreds of searchers combed the section of the rainforest where the adventure began, but to no avail. Following the map, they ventured 30 miles from their original starting point. No search effort would ever find them now.

During the entire ordeal they endured relentless insects, sleepless nights, thick thorny patches, and other predators -- the most dangerous, a pack of nearby wild boars. With each passing day the prospect of making it out alive lessened exponentially. They only started with snacks and water for a three-hour afternoon hike, not for a six-day nightmare.

On day six they hit rock bottom. There seemed no hope for getting out, so they made a suicide pact, the one choice they still controlled. Unable to walk, his companion lay exhausted in a sandy patch which was to be their final resting

Actual photo taken at the depth of despair

place. Dave traced in the sand the words "6 day lost" to identify how long they survived in the wilderness. He took a picture with his rain-soaked camera and then headed down an embankment to cleanse himself in preparation for the end.

Faith Thought: When faced with a difficult situation we tend to hunker down and try to find our own solution to the problem, often reaching the point of total exhaustion. When the situation seems hopeless there comes a time when we are tempted to give in to the inevitable. We hit rock bottom. What would you do?

Scripture: *Have I not commanded you? Be strong and courageous. Do not be afraid; do not be discouraged, for the Lord your God will be with you wherever you go (Joshua 1:9).*

Feature Story Part II: Lost in the Amazon
Thanks Be to God

A New Beginning

Their fate seemed sealed. Hopelessly lost in the Amazon rainforest, unable to walk, their tragic end seemed inevitable. Dave and his companion had agreed not to endure another night fighting insects and the uncertainty of the jungle. They wanted to end the nightmare on their own terms. In a spiritual moment, Dave decided to go down to a flooded section of the forest to "cleanse himself." When he returned from the cleansing they would put their suicide pact into action. At that moment they heard an airplane circling overhead. Because of its methodical flight pattern it was obviously searching for them. Dave marveled at the plane's freedom to fly, free as a bird, above the tree canopy. He knew they could see for miles in any direction, but he also knew there was no hope of seeing the forest floor below. The lost hikers were still trapped in the confines of the jungle. They yelled for help at the airplane in a futile attempt to be heard over the twin propellers: a hopeless gesture, but all they could do. Rescue efforts just a few hundred feet overhead were fruitless. For the moment Dave and his companion sank deeper into a feeling of helplessness, but rejuvenated by the thought that people were still looking for them.

God's plan was unfolding. At the point when Dave and his companion gave up, God took over. Like an orchestra conductor, God put all the pieces together for the rescue, setting each into action at just the right time. In His own intricate timing God had delayed the flight of the search plane for several hours until a violent thunderstorm left the area. The storm had passed. God placed a native of the area, Adenilsão, downstream at just the right time. Adenilsão was unsuccessful in his morning hunt for food for his family, so after the storm he ventured to the remote area of the rainforest where Dave and his companion were clinging to life. Paddling his crude dug-out canoe quite a distance away from the lost hikers, he nevertheless heard their desperate, futile screams at the airplane. Thanks to a radio announcement, Adenilsão knew two Americans were lost in the rainforest. He answered God's call when he heard the screams for help from many miles upstream.

God's intervention was in answer to prayer. Thousands of miles away in North Carolina, our church held prayer services for their rescue. Thanks to the speed of email we had alerted others of the desperate situation. On Sunday morning family and friends around the country were also in prayer, asking God to come to the rescue. God answered those prayers, activating all the pieces at just the perfect time. Coincidence can't take credit for the exact timing of all of the elements needed for a successful rescue.

The search plane provided a renewed hope people were looking for them. The flooded forest where Dave went to cleanse himself became the pathway out they needed. Dave helped his companion down the hill to the flooded

Actual tree where the rescue took place

forest. As they walked, the waters gradually deepened, eventually flowing into the headwaters of a river. Adenilsão, knowing two Americans were missing went back and recruited his cousin to help. They each paddled their dug-out canoes in the direction of the screams for help. After a four hour swim Dave and his companion were plucked from a tree and taken to the remote village of Alto Allegre. The villagers, who had little food or personal possessions, graciously fed and clothed them, and delicately removed the hundreds of imbedded thorns from their bodies. They sent a boat downstream to alert authorities to send a police boat to help. It was a remarkable demonstration of God's love offered by the villagers to the two lost strangers. Hours later Dave and his companion were headed for medical attention in Mauės. As they were arriving in Mauės they placed telephone calls to parents, telling of the miracle rescue. They had survived, but only because God orchestrated the rescue.

When God works miracles it is always a new beginning. The story doesn't end with the rescue, but instead sets into motion the next phase of a life's purpose. Our son became a science teacher who passionately impresses upon his middle school students an appreciation of nature's beauty, but also the importance of helping people in their time of need. His passion even earned him Teacher of the Year at his school. Dave has a renewed commitment to family, now knowing the lengths his family went to send the search plane and the network of prayers initiated by his parents. The plane was the catalyst for hope at the time of their deepest despair. It has changed our lives as parents. We have significantly increased involvement in various Christian ministries of the church, including leading mission trips to South America. As his grateful dad, it transformed me from just having my own personal faith to having the courage to boldly share that faith with others. This book is one of those public expressions of faith. We have both increased the depth of our involvement with Christian organizations. God sees the big picture. How knows how the blessings of a second chance at life will foster a renewed commitment for each of us.

After what God has done for our family, we are fully motivated to serve Him by serving others. And that is just the beginning.

Scripture: *Then I heard the voice of the Lord saying, "Whom shall I send? And who will go for us?" And I said, "Here am I. Send me!" (Isaiah 6:8).*

Question to Consider: You don't have to wait for a dramatic life-and-death situation to know that God will rally around you at your time of need. If He knows you will work to share your faith with others, he will give you that opportunity. Prepare your heart for that opportunity. If God helps you in your time of need, how would you thank Him?

Conclusion: Our God is alive today, living in the words and actions of each of us. You can see His work in the stories of this book and in the events of your life. Share your stories with others as you communicate God's love for all people.

Writer's Note: The story of their rescue has been nationally featured on two different Discovery Channel dramatizations, <u>I Shouldn't Be Alive</u> (Into the Heart of Darkness) and <u>Secrets to Survival</u> (Lost in the Amazon).

Topic: Overcoming Adversity

Overcoming Obstacles

Both the 2014 Sochi Winter Olympics and the Paralympic Games are conducted at the same venue, just a few weeks apart. Watching the Winter Olympics on television, it is easy to admire the courage, speed, endurance, and precision of the various athletes competing in the games. It is obvious the Olympic athletes work hard to reach the top of their sports.

<u>Sports Illustrated</u> magazine published pictures of Paralympic athletes, competing in many of the same events. Viewing the photos, the differences between two similar international events stood out like a sore thumb. Actually, the obstacles the Paralympic athletes overcame were Herculean. Paralympic athletes

2014 Paralympic skiers in Sochi, Russia

were missing arms and legs, but certainly weren't missing a big heart or the courage to compete. They conquered downhill slopes in a much more dramatic way than athletes with all their limbs.

Each athlete in the Paralympics has a story to tell. Some athletes lost limbs serving their country in the armed forces while others were afflicted by disease or accident. All have successfully dedicated themselves to overcoming physical obstacles in their paths. They are too busy training for success to waste time and energy lamenting the obstacles.

When bad things happen to us, do we often focus on self-pity or blaming others? Or do we save our energy for giving our best effort? While we may be motivated to overcome adversity on our own, God offers a strength that far exceeds our greatest imagination. Give God the credit and He will help you achieve your goals and be an inspiration for others. God enables people of faith to demonstrate how He can help people overcome challenges and achieve great things in His name.

Question: What examples can you give when, with God's help, you overcame obstacles and persevered to accomplish something significant?

Scripture: *So do not fear, for I am with you; do not be dismayed, for I am your God. I will strengthen you and help you; I will uphold you with my righteous right hand (Isaiah 41:10).*

Prayer: Help us, Lord, not to waste our energy thinking about the problem, but instead let us focus all our attention on the solution.

Topic: Blessings

We Blessed This Food Yesterday

My wife is an excellent cook. So, of course, I look forward to mealtime. At the end of a meal often there is some food left over for another day.

I remember a cartoon published in a newspaper some 30 years ago. A family is sitting at the dinner table with numerous bowls of food in the center of the table. The little boy, the mischievous age of Dennis the Menace, speaks up as the dad is ready to give the meal time prayer: "Do we have to say a prayer now," says the boy. "We blessed this food yesterday."

It is easy to take for granted the blessings God consistently gives us. If we are fortunate, our health is the same today as it was yesterday. Our family gathered around the dinner table today was there yesterday. If we are fortunate to be employed, the job we went to yesterday is the job we go to today. Although some things change from day to day, there are many constants in our lives. We often take these blessings for granted.

Could you imagine the overwhelming turmoil in your life if you had to start over every day and rebuild from scratch? Instead, God provides stability as the foundation in our life such as health, family, and meaningful employment, so that we have peace as we tackle the new challenges that come our way. But don't take for granted the constants in our lives. They are blessings that deserve our thanksgiving. This is a chaotic world. Be aware of the stability in your life that God lovingly provides and thank him for it. Know that His love is forever in our life and is a foundation that gives us strength to tackle what is new.

Scripture: *Every good and perfect gift is from above, coming down from the Father of the heavenly lights, who does not change like shifting shadows (James 1:17).*

Question: What blessings in your life are easy to take for granted, but provide the foundation that allows you to take on new challenges?

Prayer: Dear Lord. It is easy to take for granted the constants in our lives. We know everything we have is from you. We thank you for the many blessings you provide for us. Amen.

Topic: Making Choices

Survey Says

It is still on TV: Family Feud. They poll 100 people on possible answers to a question and then see if the contestants can name all the top possible answers on the board. The team that chooses the highest rated answer gets

control of the board, then tries to run the table by guessing the remaining survey answers. A bell rings for a correct answer and an obnoxious buzzer sounds if the answer isn't on the board: three strikes and the other team can steal the points.

Some questions are just for good-natured fun, with many possible answers.

But questions that deal with Ten Commandment issues of life don't have an array of correct answers. There should be only one answer on the board. Unfortunately, even on moral issues the audience would suggest many answers, most of which aren't biblically correct. The world rationalizes its choices, trying to tell us times have changed and there are many acceptable answers. They want to justify their answers so others will join them on the same unholy path. It is easier to go with the crowd than to do the right, biblical thing. Yet, often the crowd is wrong. On issues of morality there is only one correct answer.

Imagine if Jesus Christ was providing the answers: what would he say? Since he is the only perfect man to have ever lived on the face of this earth, we know that His choices are the right choices. In determining the answer, we should have no excuses, no rationalized answers – just follow in the path of Jesus Christ.

People actually do know what the "right" answer is, but they want to go along with the crowd. They don't want to look bad in front of others. Think of the wonderful statement you are making if people see you making the right (righteous) choice instead of the popular choice. Perhaps you can be the leader who helps others make the right choice, creating survey results based on faith.
Survey says, "Do what Jesus would do." It is not only the #1 answer, but it should be the only answer on the board.
Question: Can you go against the crowd to make choices based on faith?

Scripture: *"Why do you ask me about what is good?" Jesus replied. "There is only One who is good. If you want to enter life, obey the commandments"* (Matthew 19:17).

But be very careful to keep the commandment and the law that Moses the servant of the lord gave you: to love the Lord your God, to walk in all his ways, to obey his commands, to hold fast to him and to serve him with all your heart and all your soul (Joshua 22:5).

Prayer: Heavenly Father. The world presents us with choices to make every day of our lives. Help us to make choices based on faith, and encourage others to do the same. Amen

Topic: Seasonal/Easter

What Did You Give Up for Lent?

During the season of Lent there is a 46-day period between Ash Wednesday and Easter Sunday. The trend is to sacrificially give up something you enjoy. Many people abstain from soft drinks,  desserts, alcohol, or other things we often consume in excess or that aren't good for us in the first place. Perhaps our spouse nagged us to do this for years or perhaps we actually looked in the mirror to see our need for a change. So, for 46 days we are on good behavior, eliminating something we probably should have consumed in moderation. Our justification is its symbolic parallel to Jesus' sacrifice in the wilderness, and that He gave His life for us. There is some merit in the exercise as we consciously think about why we resist the temptation for these items.

I recently saw a Facebook post suggesting other things to "give up" during Lent. It came from a Lutheran church in New Jersey, and emphasized that the Lenten season would be more meaningful if we selected giving up things with a deeper spiritual significance.

The story listed 20, and all are traits Jesus, in His perfect life, avoided: guilt, fear, envy, impatience, sense of entitlement, bitterness and resentment, blame, gossip and negativity, comparison, fear of failure, a spirit of poverty, feelings of unworthiness, doubt, self-pity, retirement from a purposeful life, excuses, not seeking the counsel of others, pride, and worry. It is quite a list of character traits; if avoided, it would improve our relationship with God. They all involve a trust in God and putting others ahead of ourselves.

God made you to be a wonderful person. He gave you the abilities to do anything in His name. But He also gave you free will to decide whether or not you choose to live according to God's plan. Our own human nature funnels us toward the tendency to exhibit the misguided behaviors in the list above. Lent, preparing for the exhibition of God's power over sin and death, is the perfect time to try living closer to the model of Jesus' life.

On Easter Sunday, look in the mirror again. Did 46 days without soft drinks, alcohol, desserts, or whatever really make a difference? Other than perhaps losing a pound or two, are you really any different than you were the day before Ash Wednesday? Did your emulation of Jesus' sacrifice really make any difference in your life? God cares about you as a person, not the size belt you wear. In contrast, if you made an effort to give up guilt, fear, envy, and impatience, you will see a significant difference in your life. Jesus came into this world to change the world. Instead of relying on the bathroom scale to measure your willingness for change, make a conscious effort to give up a sinful behavior. You can honor His supreme sacrifice by the sacrifices you are willing to make.

Scripture: *And walk in the way of love, just as Christ loved us and gave himself up for us as a fragrant offering and sacrifice to God (Ephesians 5:2).*

Question: How does my Lenten sacrifice honor God's intent for my life?

Prayer: Heavenly Father, You showed us how to live and continually give us opportunities to be more like You. We pray we will be more intentional in honoring You with the sacrifices we make in Your name. Amen.

Bruce Boyer

Topic: Commitment

The Tell-Tale Notch in My Belt

Recently while getting ready for church, I decided to wear a dress belt. The dress belt is shiny and not de- signed to take the wear and tear of everyday use. As I tightened it to a com- fortable width I real- ized I was one notch wider than where I 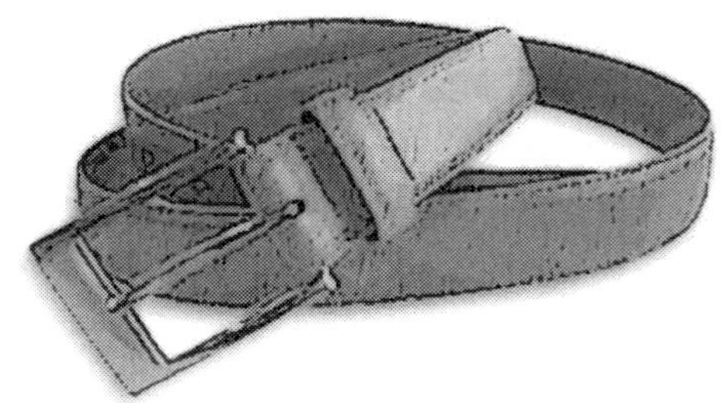 used to wear it. I was using a notch never used before. I had gained weight without even realizing it. In the busyness of my life I was oblivious to my slowly expanding waistline, but the belt provided proof that it had happened.

How are we doing with our faith walk? For many of us, we get busy with the hustle and bustle of life. We focus more on what we want to get done and don't realize an area of our lives where we are slipping. Good intentions of attending worship services, reading the Bible, and prayer – ways to strengthen our faith -- give way to other secular acts. We become consumed in checklists and the "squeaky wheel," and put the strengthening of our faith on the back burner. We convince ourselves that we'll resume faith as a priority when a big task is done. But another task follows and faith is pushed further down our priority list.

My belt casually reminded me of the wrong priority in care of my body and became an "accountability partner." Slipping in your faith is more subtle. It happens gradually over time. One way to recognize the change is to evaluate how you are spending your time. Are you making excuses why you aren't in church or reading the Bible on a regular basis? Take a look at the calendar over the past couple months and tally how many times you skipped church to do something else. Are you trying to convince yourself that you deserve to sleep in on Sunday morning or end up converting God's holy day into a time of recreation? Do you rationalize that the golf course or lake will be less crowded on a Sunday morning? Are you regularly going to the Lord in prayer or has He become an afterthought? Where is faith in your priority list? How you spend your time is the notch on your belt that reveals your priority in faith.

There is a saying, "If you think you are not as close to God as you once were, it wasn't God who moved away." God is there for you, especially during the times of your struggles. Life sometimes causes us to drift away from God a little at a time without our knowledge. Satan is sneaky that way. He doesn't want us to worship or grow our faith. Satan wants us too busy so that other things become the priority.

My belt tells me when I have "let myself go" and I may be headed for potential health problems. Find ways to monitor the commitment of your faith. Stay strong in the faith.

Scripture: *Therefore, my beloved brothers, be steadfast, immovable, always abounding in the work of the Lord, knowing that in the Lord your labor is not in vain (1 Corinthians 15:58).*

Question: Do you make excuses why you can't be in worship or take time to read the Bible? What is your top priority in life?

Prayer: Lord, it is easy to make excuses why we don't work as hard to strengthen our faith as we do other things in our lives. Help us to keep you as our priority. Amen.

Topic: Commitment

Basic Cable

Our house has basic cable – the very bottom tier subscription available: "just enough to get by," which probably fits my reputation for being frugal.

There have been times when I have sat down to watch a TV program, perhaps one that has been frequently advertised, only to find that it isn't available with my basic cable package. The message on the screen comes up, "Channel Not Available. Press 'select' to purchase." My cable channel guide is revealing. Most channels are "grayed out" as not available with my level of financial commitment. The fact is, with basic cable you don't get the good stuff.

In our daily lives, are we trying to get by with the minimum? Are we hoping to get the full complement of God's blessings but only with a half-hearted commitment on our part? Are we holding back our part of the deal, but think we fully qualify for the victory that Christ has waiting for us? We can't even click on "purchase." God's grace is not for sale at any price. God doesn't want our wallets. He wants our hearts.

He doesn't have any lower-tier grace. Heaven is as good as it gets. It is an all-or-nothing premium.

The channel of God's grace requires much more than just the bare-minimum investment. God wants the fully committed Christian – not a lukewarm person who practices faith only when there is nothing else better to do.

God's channel is a lifetime subscription that gets you everything. You can be frugal in some things, but don't hold back on how you demonstrate your faith. Give God your whole heart and He will bless you richly. Your subscription with God gets you the "good stuff."

Scripture: *But your hearts must be fully committed to the Lord our God, to live by his decrees and obey his commands, as at this time (1 King 8:61).*

Question: How are you resisting the temptation to be lukewarm in your commitment to faith?

Prayer: Lord, it is easy to do the bare minimum – just enough to get by. But we know that just getting by doesn't allow us to tune into eternal life with You. We pray we will be passionately strong in the faith.

Topic: Control

We're Still Here

One of my favorite movies is the 1983 film <u>War Games</u>. Bunkered down in the underground NORAD command center, giant monitors show missile strikes between the U.S. and Russia. The missile strikes were initiated by a teenage computer geek who

Simulated missile launches in War Games movie

found the "backdoor" into the U.S. supercomputer. What started out as playing a video game in the boy's bedroom initiated the NORAD computer's launch sequence. The command center giant screens tracked the US missile launch and Soviet retaliatory strikes. The supercomputer locked out any attempt to shut it down. A full scale global nuclear war was underway. As the supercomputer finished its visual account of the war, the world above, as we know it, would be obliterated. The command center contacted a U.S. air base in Alaska to get a report on the damage. The command center wasn't expecting a response as the air base should have been decimated by Soviet missiles. They reached a lowly airman who, with great surprise in his voice said, "Jesus H. Christ, we're still here." The war games on the screen were merely a simulation.

Looking out the window of my home also reveals we are still here. According to some people the second coming of Jesus Christ was calculated to happen May 21, 2001. Since the sun came up on May 22 we could effectively say, "We're still here." The prediction turned out to be a man-made attempt to calculate the secret hour of the second coming of Christ. No one, not even angels or Jesus Christ, knew when this would be.

Isn't that just like man – trying to take one of the most momentous promised events and predict when it would happen? We want to be in control of everything, including the actions of our God. We forget that Jesus told us, *no one knows about that day or hour, not even the angels in heaven, or the Son, but only the Father (Matthew 24:36)*. And the gospel of Mark continues with a call to action. *Be on guard! Be alert! You do not know when that time will come (Mark 13:33)*.

We want to be in control of our entire world, instead of leaving it up to God. Whose will are we seeking? Scoreboard clocks now show the remaining time of a basketball game to the tenth of a second. We send referees to the scorer's table to reset those clocks if they weren't precisely stopped at the millisecond we think they should be. It is all about control. We want to have our finger on the button, so that we have the power. As we learned in <u>War Games</u>, thankfully knowing the date of the second coming of Christ is not within our power. The final line in the movie is "The only winning move is not to play." That is good advice for us, too.

We don't know when the time will come for the end of the world, or even our own lives. We can prepare for either by living a life that shows faith made a difference. Did we use the time and resources God gave us to help others? Have we been diligent preparing to meet God? Only God can determine when each of us has finished the race and it is time to move onto eternal life. Since you are alive to read this devotion, God has given you more time to be ready for the joyous moment when you meet Him.   Take your finger off the button and give God control.

Questions: Are you using the time and gifts God gave you to help others? How is your life making a difference to others? If God came today, would you be ready to meet Him?

Prayer: Dear Lord, we pray our lives will be pleasing to You, that we are putting forth a good effort to help the less fortunate, and that we bring others with us in a quest for heaven.

Bruce Boyer

Topic: Control

Who's Driving?

I recently had an opportunity for a NASCAR Driving Experience at the Charlotte Motor Speedway. It was a gift with enough credit for me to either take the wheel for 8 laps or let four people each ride as a passenger for 3 laps with a professional driver at the wheel. I chose the latter and had three family members also share in the experience.

My own NASCAR driving expeience

If I was behind the wheel, I probably wouldn't have exceeded 100 miles per hour. Not experienced at driving high speeds, I would have been tentative as were other novices who drove their own racecar. Instead, sitting in the passenger seat, I could enjoy a ride that reached 170 mph on the straight-away with the professional driver at the wheel.

We are novices at life. Though we are attempting to maintain control, life comes at us fast. We may ride up on the heavily banked curves of life, unsure if our tires can make the curve, so we are tentative. Even if we stretch our limits and go faster than we have ever been before, we will do it with great apprehension. When we refuse to relinquish control, it's all on us.

But when Christ is in control of our lives, we can go along for the ride. He knows the course, our journey, and he knows the vehicle, our bodies. He knows what we are capable of doing. He also knows we are capable of doing much more than we allow ourselves. Should life start spinning out of control, God would be there to handle the situation. With Christ at the wheel, we cruise through life without the worry we would have if we just relied on our amateur skills at the controls. Just like the professional race car driver can accomplish more than we can, if we trust Jesus to steer our lives, we will be heading for the checkered flag.

As we were getting ready to go out on the racetrack, we had to sign a liability wavier, saying we wouldn't hold the track or its drivers responsible in case of an accident. Jesus Christ would gladly take responsibility for you, if you let Him. He holds victory over sin and death. Sign on for the ride of your life.

Life is full of a combination of sprints and curves. Let Jesus be in the driver's seat and you will accomplish much in His name.

Question: In what ways can you let Christ be at the controls of your life?

Scripture: *The Lord is my light and the one who saves me. So why should I fear anyone? The Lord protects my life. So why should I be afraid? (Psalm 27:1).*

Prayer: We pray we will give You control of our life, knowing You will never leave us or forsake us. Steer us, Lord, through the curves and obstacles of life.

Bruce Boyer

Topic: Making Decisions

Peer Pressure or Free Will

Years ago I went with a group of YMCA executives on a whitewater rafting trip. It was billed as a team-building experience to foster cooperation. The rainy October trip was on a West Virginia section of the Gauley River. A videographer accompanied our group,

Yes, I am in the rear of the raft on the Gauley River

taking action photos and videos for us to remember the trip. Prior to launch, the videographer asked some of the trip participants if they were going "of their own free will, or because of peer pressure?" Everyone interviewed on the video bravely answered, "Free will." If he had asked me, I would have truthfully said "peer pressure." All my colleagues were doing it, so I went along with the crowd. I didn't want to show my weakness.

We all have opportunities to make choices in our lives. We can hide in the crowd or we can take a stand. The crowd isn't always right. When it comes to faith, the world is often wrong. Jesus said, *Do not conform any longer to the pattern of this world, but be transformed by*

28

the renewing of your mind. Then you will be able to test and approve what God's will is – his good, pleasing and perfect will (Romans 12:2). Jesus was often doing the opposite of what people expected, and He was always right. The ways of the Lord are often different than the ways of this sinful world.

God could have made things easy for us. He could have made us to be robotically obedient all the time. Instead, He gave us free will. He gave us the ability to make choices in life. One of those choices is to believe and follow Him. What kind of commitment would it be if we automatically followed Jesus instead of following him because we truly believed with all our heart? Going along with the crowd is not a sign of strength, but of weakness. Going along with the crowd will leave you clinging to the raft for dear life because you lack the courage and faith to draw your strength from God himself. Strength of faith will help overcome the temporary cold swim as you endure the turbulent times of life. The current will eventually lead to the warmth and safety of God's loving care.

Question: Do you attend church and follow Jesus because it is expected of you, or do you honestly believe in your heart He is the Savior?

Prayer: Following the crowd will often lead us in the wrong direction. We seek to follow You, knowing it is always the right direction for our lives. Amen.

Bruce Boyer

Reality Check

All our lives we have heard that a loving Jesus would meet us in heaven, and that heaven is a beautiful place. We are told we will be reunited with loved ones in heaven and they will be free from the afflictions that made life on earth difficult for them. Those of the faith accept all these as being true: at least we say we do. But do we really believe it?

The recent movie <u>Heaven is for Real</u> is a true story about a 4-year old son of a pastor. The boy, named Colton, has an emergency surgery to remove his appendix and save his life. It does not go well and the surgeons nearly lose him on the operating table. During the operation Colton says he visits heaven, meeting Jesus and family members he never even knew on earth. Colton also meets angels who sing to him. When his father tells his congregation about his son's experiences, he gets a push-back from his church. Even though the boy's observations of heaven are consistent with the Bible, the congregation struggles to believe the story. They question if the pastor is losing his mind and needs to be replaced at the church.

Why is it OK to talk about heaven and the afterlife as if it were a fictional story, and then question the sanity of people who provide a testimony to its existence? Do we look at Jesus as a mythological character who is believable because he is the hero of the Bible, but unbelievable in real life? Are we willing to talk about heaven in the abstract but deny its existence when someone talks about it in real terms? Is it a story that is too good to be true?

Do we give lip service to heaven in church, but are afraid of what others will think about us as believers of such a sensational story? If so, are we willing to spend a lifetime in church pretending, but not really believing?

There are reality checks. An unassuming youngster clings to life on the operating table, and then recounts observations of heaven and angels. God performs a miracle, perhaps in your life. God transforms an impossible situation in an unexplainable miracle.   God gives us enough clues to take us from an unbeliever to a dedicated follower, yet we resist. God provides us with miracles, not mirages. Do you open your mind to really believe there is a loving God at work, offering you forgiveness and eternal life? Do you think it is possible that God is helping you through a situation to strengthen your faith, and helps others in theirs? Did God save Colton's life to give testimony to the existence of eternal life?

If you are open to God working through you, He will reward you with opportunities. If you truly believe in heaven, God will eventually take you there to enjoy the riches He promises to the faithful. But if, in your mind, Jesus is a character too good to be true, you won't get that opportunity. Be open when God presents you with clues. What is your reality?

Bruce Boyer

Scripture: *Faith means being sure of the things we hope for and knowing that something is real even if we do not see it (Hebrews 11:1).*

Prayer: Lord, heaven is such an unreal place that it is difficult for us to imagine it. Give us the faith to truly believe You are waiting for us in heaven.

Topic: Overcoming Fear

Your Cushion in the Storm

Friday afternoon ominous dark clouds rolled into town. A major storm was brewing. We saw it coming so we quickly turned off computers and unplugged many electrical appliances. The weather

radio automatically activated, warning us the storm was as dangerous as it looked. Within minutes the full fury of thunder, lightning, high winds and driving rain was upon us.   Lights flickered.

Once the pelting rain and electric show subsided we were faced with the aftermath. A lightning strike badly damaged the telephone line at home. Trees were toppled in the neighborhood.   Many people lost power.

Throughout our lives we are also faced with frequent storms. The world seems to come crashing down on us, bringing multiple issues all at once – seemingly too much to handle. The uncertainty brings genuine fear. Fear may come in the form of rejection, financial stress, loss of health, or relationship issues. Often we tend to let a single issue escalate into a myriad of issues, captivating our mind with what seems like an insurmountable series of problems. We make it worse by swamping our minds with endless possibilities of what could go wrong.

Bruce Boyer

One of the most familiar stories of the Bible is when Jesus was with the disciples on Lake Galilee. Jesus was asleep, resting on a cushion as a raging storm brought fear to the disciples. In fear of their lives, they awakened him. Jesus calmed the storm. Then he asked the disciples, "Where is your faith?"

That day when evening came, he said to his disciples, "Let us go over to the other side." Leaving the crowd behind, they took him along, just as he was, in the boat. There were also other boats with him. A furious squall came up, and the waves broke over the boat, so that it was nearly swamped. Jesus was in the stern, sleeping on a cushion. The disciples woke him and said to him, "Teacher, don't you care if we drown?" He got up, rebuked the wind and said to the waves, "Quiet! Be still!" Then the wind died down and it was completely calm. He said to his disciples, "Why are you so afraid? Do you still have no faith?" They were terrified and asked each other, "Who is this? Even the wind and the waves obey him!" (Mark 4:35-41).

And why does the Bible mention the cushion? A cushion is something you use to relax during your day. We can relax when Jesus is in control. Otherwise, we let problems paralyze us as fear rules our lives.

If you are a person of faith, Jesus is in the boat with you when the storms of your life come. He is ready to calm the storms, or to bring you through the storms-- if you ask. The storms of life are inevitable, but He has the power to give you peace. Let Jesus be your cushion in the face of the storms of your life.

Questions: Do you ask Jesus for help when you see storms approaching or do you try to weather them yourself and call upon Jesus only as a last resort?

Closing Prayer: Heavenly Father. We all face times in our lives when situations cause us to be afraid. Be with us. Calm the storms that attack us from all sides, and give us peace. Amen.

35

Bruce Boyer

Topic: Forgiveness

Safe at Home

Sportscenter kept showing the replay. Detroit Tigers pitcher Armando Galarraga retired the first 26 Cleveland Indians and was within one out of a rare perfect game. Only 20 perfect games had ever been recorded in Major League Baseball history. With two outs in the ninth, the batter hit a routine ground ball wide of first base. The first baseman went to his right, scooped up the ball and tossed to Galarraga, covering first base. The television announcers immediately pronounced the batter to be out,

Tiger Stadium, in Detroit

but the first base umpire surprisingly signaled safe on a close play at first. Television replays and the stadium scoreboard showed the batter clearly to be out. Nevertheless, the perfect game was over. How could this Major League umpire make a mistake, robbing Galarraga of his place in baseball immortality? To the umpire's credit, Tim Joyce realized his mistake and personally apologized to Galarraga and to the national media. In reality, the umpire thought

36

he was making the right call, and not the popular call everyone wanted to see. Two weeks later major league players voted this particular umpire to be the best in baseball. Now, that is respect for a man who made an error, but with the best of intentions.

How we react when things happen often determines the outcome. Television replays of the call at first base also show the reaction of Galarraga. He doesn't rant and rave. You don't see him mouthing words you hope your children don't see or hear. He smiles, goes back to the mound, and retires the next hitter. Game over. He wins. Isn't winning at life more important than a perfect game?

Perfection is something we simply cannot achieve in life. No matter how hard we try, we sin and are in need of God's grace. Our thoughts and deeds may be well intended, but being sinless simply is not humanly possible. Even Jesus' closest disciples sinned, and they were constantly in the presence of the Master. Think of the most pious people of faith – perhaps Billy Graham, Mother Theresa, Peter, Paul and you see wonderful people in need of a savior.

The commissioner of baseball wouldn't use the instant replay as evidence, overturn the "safe" call and award a perfect game to Galarraga. Only God can forgive our sins. When people of true faith reach the gates of heaven, God will wipe the slate clean and award a perfect game to them. Umpire Tim Joyce took responsibility for the incorrect call at first base, asking for forgiveness from the people he hurt. Jesus assumed responsibility for your sins when he died on the cross. Like Tim Joyce, we can also ask and receive forgiveness. Then, we can round the bases of life headed for home, knowing that God will reward us by calling us safe.

Scripture: *But if we confess our sins to Him, he is faithful and just to forgive us and to cleanse us from every wrong. If we claim we have not sinned, we are calling God a liar and showing that his word has no place in our hearts (1 John 1:9-10).*

Bruce Boyer

Question: How do you react when someone sins against you?

Closing Prayer: Life is far from perfect. Forgiving people who sin against us is the closest we will ever get to You, because we know You have forgiven us. Amen.

Topic: Forgiveness

Second Chance

George Jr. walked out the gate of St. Mary's Industrial School for

Babe Ruth

Boys to a waiting car. His parents had placed him in the reform school 12 years prior because he was getting into trouble constantly and often skipping school. The driver of the car was Jack Dunn, who just had been appointed George's legal guardian. Jack had seen a special talent in George and gave him a chance to make something of his life (Without George's special talent Jack would never have extended the opportunity.)

God doesn't require us to have an extraordinary talent to give us a second chance. We don't have to be worthy of the opportunity. A repentant heart and a desire to try again is all God wants us to have. When we forgive others and then ask Him for forgiveness, it is granted. God will be patient as you work through the mistakes of your life.

Our 19-year-old reform school kid was George Herman "Babe" Ruth. The iconic Babe Ruth is widely recognized as one of the greatest baseball players of all time. His 714 lifetime home runs were the most in baseball for nearly 50 years. Yet, his second chance only came because of his extraordinary talent with the bat.

You don't have to be famous in order to receive God's second, third, and fourth chances. When asked by Peter, *how many times shall I forgive my brother when he sins against me?"* Jesus said, *I tell you, not seven times, but seventy-seven times (Matthew 18:21-22).* Everyone has value to God. Let God's forgiveness be your second chance to be the best person you can be.

Question: How can you make the most of opportunities that God has provided you?

Scripture: *After you suffer for a short time, God, who gives all grace, will make everything right. He will make you strong and support you and keep you from falling. He called you to share in his glory in Christ, a glory that will continue forever (1 Peter 5:10).*

Prayer: We thank you, Lord, for the opportunity You give us to leave our shortcomings behind, start fresh, and strive to be the best we can be.

Topic: Forgiveness

Celebrating What Is Right With the World?

If someone handed to you a plain white piece of paper with one black dot on it, where would your focus go? Chances are your eyes would stare at the small black spot on the paper and not even

notice the clean white paper it is printed on. You might even be upset that a black mark spoiled a perfectly good piece of paper.

If someone wore a nice look- ing suit that had a coffee stain on it, would you admire the beautiful fabric or be distract- ed by the stain? Our tendency is to focus on the 1 percent imperfection instead of the 99 percent that is just fine. Why is it that we overlook all the good and instead dwell on the one spot of imperfection?

As imperfect people we all have many blemishes. Mankind was born into original sin. Try as hard as we can, we cannot overcome sin on our own. But we know God loves us of our sins. God forgives those who repent because Jesus died on the cross for us.

Bruce Boyer

I recently saw a video entitled <u>What is right with the world</u>. The narrator, Dewitt Jones, is a world class photographer from <u>National Geographic</u> magazine. The video showed an image of a single flower sprouting up in a wheat field. To the farmer, the flower is a blemish; but to the photographer, it is the featured part of the photo. We can learn from that concept, and love people because of their uniqueness.

In a healthy marriage, spouses kid each other about imperfections. Couples in a healthy marriage love each other in spite of their shortcomings. We love others because God first loved us. And he died on the cross so we can be forgiven all our sins.

Celebrate the beauty of a person's uniqueness. We are made in God's image. Express your love to people as you enjoy what makes them special.

Don't be hard on yourself because you know your own shortcomings. You are a creation of God and a very special person because of it. You are one of the things that is right with the world.

Scripture: *Above all, love each other deeply, because love covers over a multitude of sin. (1 Peter 4:8).*

Question: What makes you special?

Prayer: You have made each of us to be a unique individual. Help us to appreciate what makes others special and to overlook their shortcomings. Amen.

Topic: Friendship

And She Closed the Lid on the Piano

My daughter teaches voice lessons in New York City. Aspiring actors set up one-hour appointments to work on their vocal techniques, often in preparation for Broadway auditions or touring shows. The world of an actor is a difficult one. They feel pressure for a successful audition to earn the right to work for just a month or  two, and then start all over again with the next show. Their world is one of frequent rejection by casting directors who may listen to the singer for just a few seconds before sending them on their way with a simple "thank you very much." And all that is after a six-hour wait for their 30 seconds of singing for the casting director. Consequently, a student's self-esteem can be very fragile.

There are times when my daughter's students show up for their appointment and indicate their biggest need is for a "therapy lesson" instead of a voice lesson. Kara immediately closes the lid on the piano and gives her full attention to the personal needs of the student. Not a note is sung but the student leaves an hour later with a clearer direction and a sense of peace.

Bruce Boyer

Are we ready to close the lid on our pianos when someone needs our undivided attention? Can we put aside our plans and respond to the needs of someone else when they are fragile and vulnerable. Closing the lid, setting aside the work on the desk or putting down the morning paper is a clear sign that we are ready to listen to the needs of the other person. The easy advice is telling the person what you would do, but the most helpful approach is conveying what God would do in their situation. Human responses often involve providing the answer we think they want to hear. God's advice is the perfect answer.

God is ready to do that for you, too. No appointment is necessary. Just open up to God and tell Him what is on your heart, then listen for His advice. The Bible also gives God's advice as well. Set aside some time each day to read his Word and for dialogue with Him. God will close the lid on His piano and give you His full attention, helping you find direction and a sense of peace.

Question: How do you give your full attention when people wish to talk with you for advice?

Scripture: *Peace I leave with you; my peace I give you. I do not give to you as the world gives. Do not let your hearts be troubled and do not be afraid (John 14:27).*

Prayer: We thank you, Lord, for Your willingness to listen. We pray we will be open to Your answers.

Topic: Seasonal/Christmas

A Light for You

During the Christmas season, power bills skyrocket but the atmosphere around the neighborhood is bright and festive. Outdoor Christmas lights are spread through shrubbery and lining the roofline of homes. Illuminated manger scenes and lighted, moving reindeer add to the holiday atmo-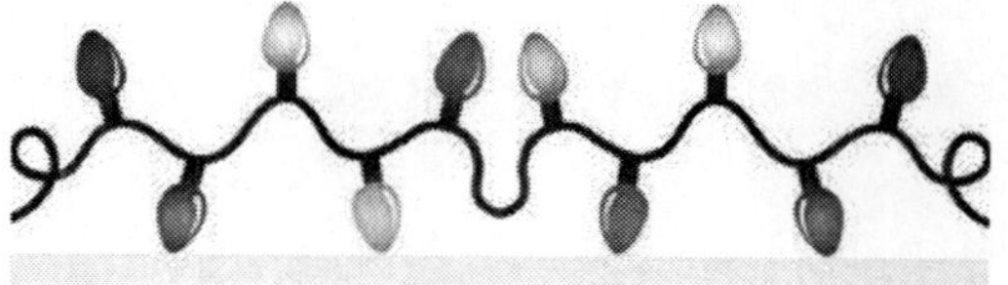sphere. Blow-ups spring up in the front lawn. Some light strands even play Christmas music. Inside, hundreds of lights illuminate the Christmas tree, with a special angel or star at the top. Christmas villages, window candles, and other decorations light up, cast a warm glow throughout the house. It's beginning to look a lot like Christmas.

Christmas time is a symbolic time for showing the light of Christ, but we can do this year-round.

Scripture tells us to show our light for others to see. If Christ is in your life, you can be an inspiration to others. *You are the light of the world. A town built on a hill cannot be hidden. Neither do people light a lamp and put it under a bowl. Instead they put it on its stand, and it gives light to everyone in the house. In the same way, let your light shine before others, that they may see your good deeds and glorify your Father in heaven (Matt 5:14-16).*

Not only can we decorate for the season, but we have many opportunities to do good deeds that glorify God. The second part of that statement is critical. When people see our motivation to be serving and glorifying God, they are encouraged to do the same. That is the light Jesus wants us to shine for others to see. God is illuminated *through you.*

Scripture: *Jesus said to the people, I am the light of the world. If you follow me, you won't be stumbling through the darkness, because you will have the light that leads to life (John 8:12).*

There is nothing more important we can do than to bring others to Christ, helping them to see a better life through Jesus. In Acts 13:47, the Lord said, I have made you a light to the Gentiles, to bring salvation to the farthest corners of the earth.

Let's light up the neighborhoods and our homes – not only at Christmas time, but throughout the year. Perhaps we can help keep someone from stumbling in the dark. Better yet, someone may achieve salvation because of the light we shine.

Question: In what ways can you share the light of Christ with others?

Prayer: We thank you, Lord, for showing us the light that leads to salvation. We pray that we can help others to come from darkness into that light.

Topic: Grace

Free at Last

Do you remember? "I have a dream, that one day this nation will rise up and live out the true meaning of its creed: We hold these truths to be self-evident, that all men are created equal." Dr. Martin Luther King Jr. dreamed a country founded on freedom, justice, and equality would live up to its founding principles. Dr. King's passionate speech challenged a nation to be what it was founded to be. In 1963, our country clearly was far short of equality for all men.

Dr. Martin Luther King, Jr.

Dr. King didn't write the founding principles of the United States. He was 200 years too late for that, but with deep passion he urged an entire nation to embrace the quest for freedom.

As a Christian, do you have a dream? Is your dream that your friends and family will enjoy the freedom that Jesus won for us? None of us living today wrote the manuscript, but we can be the messenger that shares it with others. The Bible, written some 2,000 years ago, describes an offer of God's grace – freedom from the punishment our sins deserve.   We are free to live in the freedom Jesus won for us.

Dr. King's speech was delivered on the steps of the Lincoln Memorial during a particularly tumultuous time in our country's history. Today we also live in a difficult time. Never has our country been as fractured and in as much moral decay. The time is right for Christians of all walks of life to step forward and be advocates for the kind of loving world God intended. The Bible, U.S. Constitution, and the Emancipation Proclamation are the foundation upon which freedom is built.

Our world this side of heaven will never be perfect. The redeeming message is we can be free from sins because of God's grace. When this happens, we can all say, "Free at last! Free at last! Thank God Almighty, we are free at last!"

Question: Are you willing to be a messenger for Christ and share your dream for eternal freedom?

Scripture: *If we confess our sins, He is faithful and just to forgive us our sins and to cleanse us from all unrighteousness (1 John 1:9).*

Prayer: We thank you, Lord, for the freedom you have won for us. Thank God Almighty, we are free at last. Amen.

Topic: Grounded in Faith

Gravity

Sandra Bullock won the 2014 Academy Award for Best Female performance, in the sci-fi movie <u>Gravity</u>. Much of the 3-D movie showed the two characters floating around in space, both inside and outside a space capsule. Drifting in space, without the grounding effect of gravity, there is no "up or down." Everything floats around  aimlessly unless held in place by something. On Earth, gravity keeps us invisibly tethered to the planet and holds our water and air supply in place. Gravity supports life as we know it.

In the movie, a nearby satellite explodes sending space debris on a collision course with the space shuttle of the movie's main two characters, Dr. Ryan Stone and Matt Kowalski. At one point in the movie, Stone and Kowalski are tethered to nothing but each other and spiraling out into the blackness of outer space. Communication from Mission Control in Houston is cut off. The astronauts have no idea if Mission Control can hear their outgoing messages. The characters try different attempts to repair their crippled ship, which is quickly losing its oxygen supply. The movie description says, "They are often on their own without the other leading to an extreme feeling of isolation which leads to individual questions and ultimate decisions about their own mortality…"

That describes people without faith. Without two-way communication with the God who loves them, they are on their own, living in the darkness of the unknown. There is no grounding effect on their decision-making. They live in isolation, trying to survive with their own limited abilities and without spiritual knowledge of right and wrong. We all know that worldly opinions of right and wrong are based on public opinion and personal gain, far from a biblical grounding. Mortality takes on a totally different meaning for people without faith. People without faith live in a vacuum that does not support life.

Faith is our "gravity," using its powerful force to align all aspects of life in proper perspective. God is the force, drawing us toward Him. *Even there your hand will guide me, your right hand will hold me fast (Psalm 139:10).* God created gravity to hold our world and all its life-giving essentials in place. Science acknowledges gravity accomplishes its purpose perfectly, establishing just the right strength to do its job here on Earth. The movie plot is a science-fiction story but depicts accurately what it would be like to be drifting aimlessly in space. The story's characters didn't know if Mission Control could hear their pleas for help, but we know that God hears, and He will respond. Let your life be guided by the spiritual force that keeps you grounded in the faith.

Question: How do you stay grounded in the faith when life on Earth takes so many twists and turns, seemingly spinning out of control?

Scripture: *Since you are my rock and my fortress, for the sake of your name, lead and guide me (Psalm 31:3).*

Prayer: We thank You, Lord, for being the invisible gravity in our lives as we explore the opportunities of Christian service in our communities. We pray we will always be grounded in our faith.

Bruce Boyer

I Hope to Ask Him Someday
"One Eternal Generation of Christians"

When my mom had a devastating stroke, we took advantage of the little time we had left to make sure we told her we loved her. We

Moses with the 10 Commandment tablets

also wanted to be sure her heart was right -- not physically, but that it was right with God. My goal was to make sure she understood where she, because of her faith, was going. But from the moment of her stroke, she lost the ability to respond to us. The opportunity for two-way dialogue would have to wait.

Ray Vanderlaan has produced a series of DVD faith lessons. I was struck by a casual comment Ray made in one of the videos as he sought to more deeply understand a moment in biblical history. His remark was that he had a question he would like to ask Moses. He said, "I hope to ask him someday." That was such a simple but profound statement. A person of our time wants to talk with someone who lived some 3,500 years ago. Because of the resurrection of Jesus Christ and the promise that people of faith will have eternal life, we will be able to talk with people who have passed into the next life before and after us. In the next life there is only one generation of Christians.

Do you have friends or loved ones of faith who have gone on before you? Are there things you wish you had said to them? Do you have questions you would like to ask? What would my Mom say after hearing those closing, reassuring words?

There are events in life when people are instantly taken away from us, and we don't get the chance for final goodbyes. People of faith don't have to worry about the goodbye part. Goodbyes are only for the world in which we live. Knowing we can see loved ones again is another benefit of having faith in the living God who assures us of our place in eternity.

Are there people in your life you want to be with forever? While we are living the current life we should do everything possible to be sure others also benefit from God's promise of eternal life. Then the time of memorial services is more of a celebration of life because we know where they are headed.

Question: What question do you wish to ask someone in the next life?

Scripture: *And this is the will of God, that I should not lose even one of all those he has given me, but that I should raise them to eternal life at the last day. For it is my Father's will that all who see his Son and believe in him should have eternal life—that I should raise them at the last day (John 6:39).*

Prayer: We thank you, Lord, for the gift of eternal life. We know we will be united with loved ones forever.

Bruce Boyer

Topic: Hope

The King Has One More Move

In the game of chess, players seem to know when a game is lost.

 Instead of being beaten by their opponent they often resign the game. They give up. They quit. In their thinking, quitting is preferable to the opponent having the joy of making the winning move.

Look around at the world we live in. Every decade has its share of unwinnable wars. How do we rationalize situations where people become human bombs in large crowds, taking the lives of innocent people? Do you remember the feeling of helpless despair felt on September 11, 2001? Our country is full of unsettling events beamed into our living rooms every day. The sum total of these events saps our energy and creates a feeling of hopelessness.

If the devil is behind all this, is he winning? Is there hope for people who care about others in this world? Human needs seem far greater than our ability to solve all the world's problems. Still, because of our faith, we have hope. We know that God will not forsake us.

A young man named Bobby Fischer was in the audience of a major chess tournament match. Fischer would eventually become one of the world's best chess players ever. On this day, as one player was ready to resign, Bobby shouted, "The game is <u>not</u> over. The king has one more move." Bobby could see, with greater perspective, there was a winning move. Instead of defeat, victory was imminent.

The game is not over. As humans we may not see a solution but there is a greater vision that shows us the game is not over.

No matter how bleak the times seem to be, no matter how disappointed we are with the events in our world and personal life, the King – our Lord God Almighty -- has the final move. God's final move is the hope we have in our Savior being fulfilled. God is going to win. Satan knows he is destined to lose, but wants to take as many of us down with him as he can. That is why it is important that we not give up or let down. The power of positive thinking is not fooling ourselves that there are no problems in this world, but instead to live and act with confidence that God will win in the end. The righteous will prevail. With a cheerful, encouraging heart, we can help the people around us who are in need. The King has one more move. Checkmate.

Scripture: *I am the Alpha and the Omega, the Beginning and the End, the First and the Last. Blessed are those who do His commandments, that they may have the right to the tree of life, and may enter through the gates into the city (Revelation 22: 13-14).*

Question: When things are bleak how can you give God the chance to make the winning move?

Prayer: We can't see the future, Lord, so it is easy to give up on seemingly hopeless situations. But You are our hope. Let us trust that You have answers to all the situations we may face. Amen.

Bruce Boyer

Topic: Hope

Numb3rs

One of the most intriguing television shows of the last decade is Numb3rs (spelled correctly according to the TV show). The show is about a young mathematician genius who helps his older brother, an FBI agent, solve all kinds of crimes in the Los Angeles area. The star of the show uses complicated mathematical calculations that determine probability theories to solve the mystery. Formulas are displayed in line after line of calculations written on grease boards and clear plastic walls. It is amazing what numbers can do to unravel the case at hand. In the TV series, every case is solved when the right formula is used.

I have a better formula to suggest. It is a formula that will unravel mystery and reveal the solution to times of despair. Instead of a complex formula, it all boils down to 3 simple digits, 3-1-6. In Max Lucado's book <u>3:16</u> the author substitute nails for the colon. After all, Jesus was the substitute for us on the cross at Calvary.

By now those numbers are becoming clear to you. They are the numbers of hope: *For God so loved the world that he gave his one and only Son, that whoever believes in him shall not perish but have eternal life (John 3:16).*

Crime-fighting shows analyze what happened and determine motive. God's motive is "love." Because of God's great love for mankind He gave us His son to die on the cross. Jesus suffered pain in the hope that He can reduce our pain. Jesus suffered death, followed by the resurrection so that we might have eternal life. As you expect, most Hollywood stories have the good guys winning in the end. They certainly do in God's story.

We have a role in John 3:16. Compared to God's sacrificial role, all we have to do is believe. There is no equal sign in the formula as God gives so much more than we could possibly give. Knowing there is a happy ending, believing is a no brainer. It is clearly written in the script. If you need proof, you can fast forward and see how the mathematical formula in the TV show solves the case. If you need proof in real life, fast forward to the book of Revelation. The good guys win in real life, too. Make no mistake about it – the numbers 3-1-6 save lives. Our part in the story also involves sharing our faith with others, in hopes they will also become believers. There is no mathematical probability involved. God's love for us is an absolute value. Case solved.

Question: Do you believe in eternal life for all believers and are you willing to encourage others to believe, also?

Prayer: We thank you Lord for the gift of your son, so that we may have hope for eternal life.

Bruce Boyer

Where Do You See God?

Sometimes I see Facebook posts of clouds or other images where,

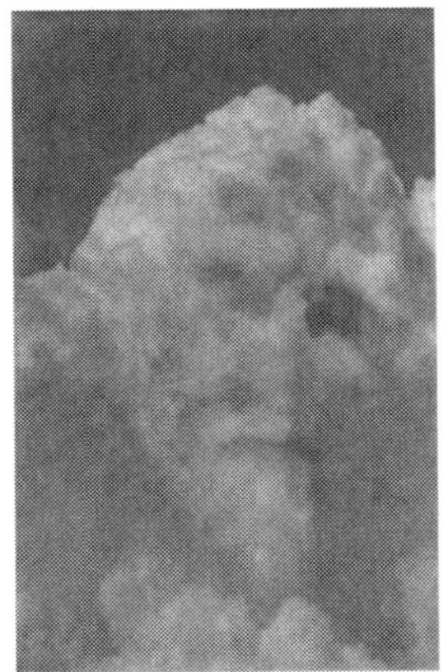

if you look hard enough, you can see the face of Christ. His loving face is unmistakable and sometimes appears at the most opportune time.

God, the creator of our universe, is everywhere and there every time we need him. You just need to seek Him. He is at the

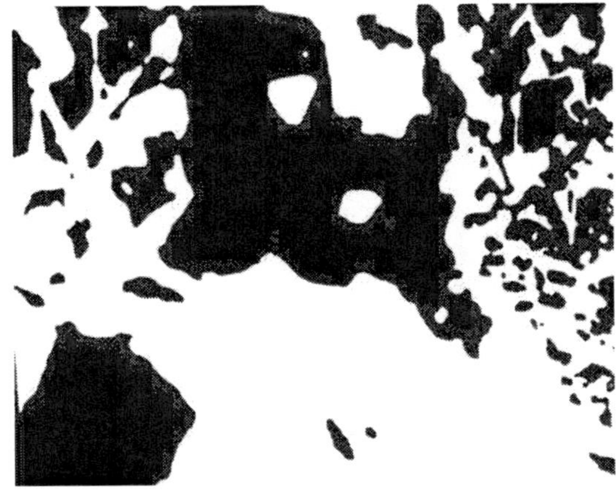

other end of your prayers. He is in your hearts and minds, just waiting to interact with you. God is within other people who love you and want to help you and are serving God because of their faith.

Christ's face in the snow

Yes, God is whenever and wherever you need Him to be.

It takes little imagination to see visuals of our Lord and Savior, Jesus Christ. God chooses when He wants to reveal himself to each of us, often in a unique way to each person. He reveals himself to us in a way we can understand. Not everyone can look at an image and see Christ. It may take several minutes to point out key features that help others see God's image. The familiar verse, *So God created man in his own image, in the image of God he created him; male and female he created them (Genesis 1:27)*, is about the character and attributes of God. It is not a true-to-life digital picture you can print out. We can reflect the character of God through actions that display our faith. Let God act through you. You can be his hands and feet. You can share His love.

Look for God throughout your everyday life – physically and in the events of your day. God is always near you and wants to reveal Himself and His hopes for your life. Perhaps you can be the person who helps others see God in their lives.

Question: In what ways has Christ revealed Himself to you at unexpected times, places, or circumstances?

Prayer: Heavenly Father, we look for your daily presence in our lives. We pray you will be the guiding force in all we do, and that we will help others to see you. Amen.

Bruce Boyer

Topic: Joy

A Spring in Your Step

Our church often enjoyed a musical cantata during the Advent sea-

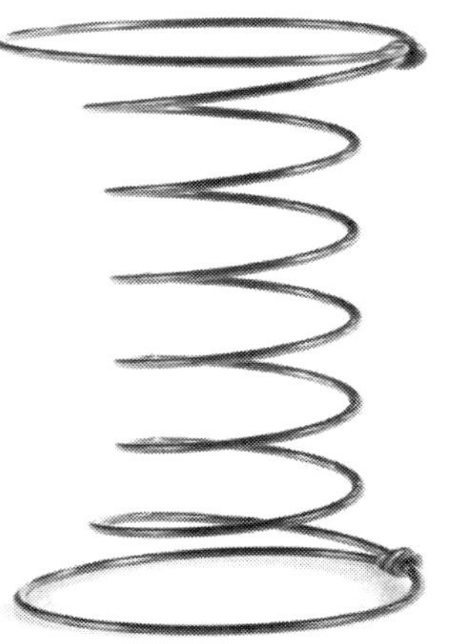

son. The cantata was a 30-min-
ute presentation of music and
narration that tells the Christmas story. Most of it consisted
of musical arrangements of familiar Christmas carols, but sung
like a ballad – smooth and sentimental. There was one song,
however, that was very much
different. The song, "'Tis a
Wonderful Thing," is a spiritual
song played with a jazzy swing
feel. The trumpet accompaniment created a "big band" counter-
melody that jazzed up a song. The upbeat song was played near
the end of the cantata. At its conclusion, the service continued
with prayers, communion and the benediction. As the congregation started to leave, the choir did a reprise of the peppy song as
a postlude.

That's when the fun began. Many members of the congregation
immediately broke into a dance step. Seven or eight people were
strutting around to the beat of the music, invigorated by the music
and feeling the freedom to express their up-tempo mood. Even
though everyone was still in the sanctuary, there was no need to

remain stoic and reserved. It was time to celebrate and have fun.

Because of our faith we can go out into the world with "a spring" in our step. We don't need music to swing us into action. The communion shared at that service allowed us to know we are forgiven so that we are not burdened with regret for anything that happened that week. Plus, God invites us to lay down our troubles at the altar so that our load is lighter. Thirdly, Jesus encourages us to serve God by serving others so that we can be invigorated as we help others. It is no wonder why we can have a spring in our step as we leave worship and begin another week with a newly recharged spirit.

The postlude may enliven the sanctuary but God wants you to dance in your heart even when there is no music playing. "Tis a wonderful thing."

Question: Do you dance out of church with a sense of rejuvenation? Do you allow yourself to feel your burdens have been lifted off your shoulders? Does communion allow you to wipe the slate clean with God and start fresh again?

Scripture: *God will fill your mouth with laughter and your lips with shouts of joy (Job 8:21).*

Bruce Boyer

Topic: Joy in Serving

Make a Joyful Noise Unto the Lord

Years ago I sat next to Don for the first time at a worship service. He had been very active at church for several years and was a great servant of the Lord.

During the service, he stepped out of the sanctuary for a mo-ment. When he came back in, we were just preparing to sing the final hymn. As he picked up the hymnal, I could tell he was trying to find the right spot on the page to resume singing along with the rest of the congregation. It was important to him to be fully engaged in worship by singing the words to the hymn. During every response, song of praise, or prayer I could see his mouth move to participate actively with the rest of the congregation.

Why is this so motivating to me? The man had no voice box. He could only be audibly heard when he held a device up to his throat to amplify the sound. During the worship service he didn't use the device, but he still sang with all the gusto of the best tenor in the choir. He didn't let anything stop him from fully worshipping and serving the Lord.

62

Stories of Faith from Everyday Life

In our lives it is easy to come up with excuses why we can't serve in some capacity or fully participate in worship. Our excuses are often related to what we don't want to do rather than what we can't do. Most of us don't have the physical limitations that my friend had. Yet, the person in our congregation who physically couldn't be heard spoke to my heart a message so loud and clear that I couldn't help but hear it.

Do you make excuses that prevent you from having an impact on others? Do you stay home on a Sunday morning just because you are tired?

We can learn from worshipping side by side with someone who has every reason to make an excuse, yet overcomes obstacles to epitomize the essence of a true servant. God heard my friend's voice that day and so did I. God works through people to be a source of motivation for all of us. If you let Him, God will work through you.

Question: Do people see your love for Jesus, or do your words get in the way'?

Scripture: *Oh come, let us sing to the Lord; let us make a joyful noise to the rock of our salvation! (Psalm 95:1).*

Closing Prayer: Lord, we pray that we won't make excuses why we won't serve or worship you. Let us place service and worship as a top priority in our lives. Amen.

Bruce Boyer

Topic: Seasonal/Valentine's Day/Love

And the Greatest of These Is ...

We all know the final word in the passage from 1 Corinthians 13:13. It is etched in our minds and our hearts. If anyone says the first six words and pauses, we automatically fill in the 7th. And the greatest of these is "Love."

Valentine's Day is full of expectations. On the day set aside for expressing our love, we give our loved ones a combination of flowers, dinner, jewelry and candy. My wife and I exchange boxes of candy each year, a two-way exchange of mutual love.

Love is powerful because it goes both ways. God is the best example of mutual love. *We love because he first loved us (1 John 4:19).* God takes the gift of love to the limit in his sacrificial love. *My command is this: Love each other as I have loved you. Greater love has no one than this that he lay down his life for his friends (John 15:12-13).* Jesus demonstrated this love when he laid down his life for his friends – you and me. That is much more significant than a box of candy or a pendant from a jewelry store. He gave it all for you, and for me.

Love is the most common word in the Bible, and perhaps it should be the most common word in our vocabulary and actions. Several years ago a TV commercial aired about a man who couldn't say "I love you" to his girlfriend. He would stutter and then chicken out, saying that he loves other objects, but balked at saying the specific words "I love you." Those words make a commitment, something God has already given to you. God frequently expresses his love for us. Hopefully, we won't balk at telling God of our love for him. It is, after all, a mutual commitment.

God doesn't give heart-shaped boxes of candy, yet His gift is even sweeter. The heart-shaped candy boxes add warmth to our feelings about people, and yes, calories to our waist lines. God's gift to you comes in a different shape – that of a cross. It is a commitment that contains no calories, just sacrificial love.

As kids we used to send cards that said, "Be My Valentine." God already sent you a Valentine, the life of His Son, Jesus Christ. Now it is our turn to respond because He first loved us. No postage is required for delivery. Ask God to be your Valentine through prayer.

God's love is everlasting. *And now these three remain: faith, hope and love. But the greatest of these is love (1 Corinthians 13:13).* The box of candy is consumed in days; God's love lasts forever.

Let every day be Valentine's Day between you and God. It is the greatest gift of all time for all time.

Question: Have you told God of your love for Him?

Prayer: We love you, Lord. We thank you for the gift of your son and promise to love others because you first loved us.

Bruce Boyer

Topic: Love

The Trick Candle

Have you ever been to a birthday celebration where there is a trick candle on the cake? Try as hard as you like, the candle can't be blown out. It may sputter and flicker, but then it will come back to life just as bright as it was before. The flame burns deep within the candle and not just on the surface.

You can tell if a cake has a trick candle on it. All the other candles just burn until the wax and wick are gone, or until the slightest breeze snuffs them out. The trick candle has that extra sparkle when it burns.

That is how it is with God's love. We can do or say things that are not pleasing to God, but His love comes back just as strong as it was before. God loves us deeply so that the real flame is protected from the problems on the surface of our lives.

The popular Christian song, entitled "Pass It On" talks about God's love: "That's how it is with God's love; once you've experienced it, you want to pass it on." Share that love with others. We can love others because God first loved us. It is a love that transcends the daily problems and can't be extinguished. It sparkles. God loves us for who we are. We can do the same as we pass it on.

Scripture: *For I am convinced that nothing can ever separate us from His love. Death can't and life can't. The angels won't, and all the powers of hell* *itself cannot keep God's love away (Romans 8:38).*

Question: What times in your life did you feel that the flame of faith was nearly extinguished, yet came back to life? How did it make you feel knowing that God was with you during your darkest hours?

Prayer: Heavenly Father, we all experience times when our faith flickers and nearly goes out. We thank You for never giving up on us, allowing our faith to spring back to life as strong as ever before. Help us to share that faith with others.

Bruce Boyer

Topic: Patience

Play On

Soccer is a game of continuous motion. When played at a high level, it is a fluid 90-minute match, with as few whistles (stoppages of play) as possible. If you are close enough to the field you'll often hear the center referee yell "Play on." The referee makes a gesture with his arms that indicates play is to continue, in spite of an infraction that just happened. The casual spectator may

Soccer referee instructional photo for "Play On"

get incensed at this no-call, seeing a player fall to the ground as a result of an obvious foul, yet no whistle sounds. Seconds later the same spectator often says something to this effect: "It's a good thing the team scored on the play because the stupid referee missed an obvious foul." Little did the spectator know the referee saw the ball go directly to another teammate who was in position to make a play on goal. He held his whistle to allow something more significant to happen.

The referee saw the big picture, and knew it was better for the fouled team to continue advancing the ball downfield. Something good might happen, and certainly the opportunity has better potential for a positive result than if play had been instantly stopped.

It is a good thing our Lord and Savior doesn't have a quick whistle when evaluating our lives. God sees the big picture. He knows what is in store for us downfield. He even knows where our teammates are who may pick up the pieces and be in a position to accomplish an even bigger goal than we imagined. He knows that if we play through some of the issues in our lives, because of our faith, we will succeed.

God's game plan for our lives is perfect, and may be entirely different from what we imagine. It takes our trust in Him to wait for the right decision, leading to the right outcome. The fouled player may want the quick whistle as instant vindication for the opposing player's reckless tackle. Yet, if we trust the referee's (God's) judgment, we will win in the end. Swallow your pride and stubbornness and look up to watch the ball go in the net. Celebrate the victory Christ has won for you. GOOAAAAAL!

Question: Can you play through temporary hardships to see God's plan unfold for your life?

Scripture: *We also have joy with our troubles, because we know that these troubles produce patience. And patience produces character, and character produces hope. And this hope will never disappoint us, because God has poured out his love to fill our hearts (Romans 5:3-5).*

Prayer: Give us the patience, Lord, to overcome the obstacles in our paths so that we will discover your plan for our lives.

Bruce Boyer

Topic: Perseverance

Victory Against Any Odds

Athletic competition creates some fascinating storylines. An underdog team playing against a dynasty is a mecca for storylines. Teams that never seem to lose have their loyal fan base, yet even the mighty teams will eventually taste defeat. It has been said, "The bigger they are, the harder they fall." But the underdog is often the sentimental favorite. Cheering for the underdog is  such a popular thing to do. Sports movies often highlight teams like the <u>Bad News Bears</u>, who overcome seemingly insurmountable odds to win the once-in-a-lifetime championship. Remember the "Miracle" US hockey victory in the 1980 Olympics or tiny Milan High School's Indiana state basketball championship in the movie <u>Hoosiers</u>. "Do you believe in miracles? Yes!" In each storyline, winning as the underdog was euphoric, especially when defeating a perennial winner. Fans of the underdog appreciate and remember the specialness of victory much more than those who feel "entitled" to win.

Paul wrote in Romans 5:3-5, *And we rejoice in the hope of the glory of God. Not only so, but we also rejoice in our sufferings, because we know that suffering produces perseverance; perseverance character; and character hope.*

And then Paul goes one step further when he says, *And hope does not disappoint us because God has poured out his love into our hearts by the Holy*

Spirit, whom he has given us (Romans 5:6).

In many respects sports is a world of fantasy. Real life is the arena where Christians seem to fight an uphill battle. The cards seem to be stacked against us. God doesn't promise the believer an easy life, but He does promise an eventual victory. There will be bumps and bruises along the way, but that is part of the strengthening process of overcoming evil in the world. God encourages us to persevere because He will be with us always, to help us through the difficult times. *And surely, I am with you always, to the very end of the age (Matthew 28:20).*

Jesus teaches us to persevere, to be of good character and then we have the assurance for life eternal. With God's help, overcoming challenges makes us stronger, and we appreciate the accomplishment even more. Stay the course, trust God for strength, and use His power to overcome all obstacles. Then you can enjoy the specialness of victory. We know the victory will come, and with it life eternal. Enjoy the journey.

Question: What times in your life did you persevere through tough times and were blessed with success?

Prayer: Lord, we all seek victory, and we realize that true victory comes with sacrifice, commitment, faith and perseverance. Help us to be patient as we seek the ultimate victory.

Bruce Boyer

Topic: Prayer

You've Got Mail

I spent 13 summers as a camper or counselor at YMCA camp.

During those days mail was handed out in the dining hall at lunch time. A staff member would call out campers' names and they would go up to get their letters. That was one of the best walks of the day. You knew the letter was from someone who loved you – usually a parent or special friend.

My parents gave me the opportunity to be at camp nearly all summer, an environment I thoroughly enjoyed. Sometimes I enjoyed things so much I let my own letter writing slide. One late summer day, mail call came and sure enough, my name was called. When I picked up the letter I recognized immediately it was from home. But when I opened up the envelope I pulled out a blank piece of paper, nicely folded, but with no message on it. My parents, in their own not-so subtle way, were telling me that dialogue was supposed to be two-way. I wasn't doing my part.

How is your dialogue with God? Is it two-way? Are you listening as well as talking? Or, are you too busy at times to even spend time in prayer each day?

The way my parents handled the lack of a letter from me got my attention. The blank piece of paper said, in essence, we are still here and still love you. We want to be part of your life if you just let us in. When we don't communicate with God, He is thinking the same thing. He is still there, waiting in love for dialogue with us. He wants to be part of our life. He wants to hear about our daily activities and struggles we may be facing.

God is waiting for His name to be called out, as you seek communication with him. When you talk with God you can count on a heavenly reply that certainly is not a blank piece of paper. God's reply will be full of blessings. God loves you either way, but He enjoys the communication from you. Don't let the busyness of life distance you from God. Someday, you want Him calling out your name, saying He has a letter waiting for you. You've got mail.

Scripture: *Jesus said, 'Until now you have not asked for anything in my name. Ask and you will receive, and your joy will be complete' (John 16:24).*

Question: Is God still waiting to hear from you? When did you last spend time communicating with your Lord and Savior?

Prayer: This devotion is all about a frequent dialogue with God. Rather than suggesting a prayer, take a moment of silence to talk to God about your day and listen for his response.

Bruce Boyer

Steering Wheel or Spare Tire

The spare tire on my car is hidden under the floorboard in the rear of the vehicle. Some cars and trucks mount the spare tire un-

der the vehicle, requiring you to craw under it to release the tire. Not very convenient, is it? In either case the spare tire is kept out of sight, out of mind. How often do you check you spare tire's air pressure? Not often, I would guess. Yet, it serves a very important purpose: keeping you moving if something happens to one of the other four tires. It rescues you when needed, but otherwise it is not used at all. You forget it is there.

The steering wheel, on the other hand, is what controls the direction of the car. It is essential in everthing we do with the car. Without the steering wheel, the car would careen out of control.

A recent Facebook posting stated, "Prayer should be your stering wheel, not your spare tire." Do you only call on God to get you out of a jam? Is God your emergency spare tire that is only recalled when you blow a tire? Otherwise, it is relegated to the trunk. Chances are it has great tread because it hasn't been used.

In effect, you are saying to God, "I'll call you when I need you. The rest of the time, I will essentially ignore you - but you had better be ready when disater comes." That is a weak relationship with God. Even the term "spare" implies it is an unnecessary extra that you could live withour most of the time.

If you look at prayer as your steering wheel, you will be in frequent communication with God. You will be asking God to guide you every inch of the way, regardless of whether your life is going forward or backward. Not all of life is full speed ahead. Sometimes you need to go backward to be in a position to move forward. God steers your direction even in reverse. He wants to be a part of your everyday life, not just an afterthought.

God can help you out of jams but he wants to be with you in the front seat of the car. Going to him often in prayer will significantly reduce the jams you encounter. As human beings, we often start off in the wrong direction. He'll steer you in the right direction. God's direction for your life is perfect.

Can you imagine the difference in the Lord's impact in your life if you are in costant communication with him, rather than locking him in the trunk? Let God steer your life.

Scripture: *The Lord makes me lie down in greeen pastures, he leads me beside quiet waters; he restores my soul. He guides me in paths of righteousness for his name's sake (Psalm 23:2-3).*

Question: Where is God in your life? Is He in the front seat steering you in the right direction, or locked in the truck, forgotten untl your life has gone flat?

Prayer: Father, we ask you to be the daily guide in our lives, steering us in the right direction. We surrender our life to You and welcome Your guidance. Amen.

Bruce Boyer

Topic: Priority of Faith

A Patch of Dirt

We take pride in keeping our lawn green and healthy. To help accomplish this we put in a sprinkler system that is set to water the lawn every morning. Even during the course of a dry summer the lawn looks reasonable, except for one small patch. There is one very small section of grass between our driveway  and that of our neighbor. It is too small an area to put in a sprinkler, so when the dry summer comes it receives nourishment only when we intentionally hand-water the area. Like most people, we have very busy schedules so watering this patch is very intermittent. As a result, our lawn has a healthy stand of grass... except for this one area.

Isn't that the way things are with life? Our faith receives some nourishment during the good times. When that happens we stay healthy spiritually. At other times – perhaps when we are stressed, overworked and feeling down - we let down and do not feed our faith. Other priorities take up our time and attention. If we ignore the daily care our faith needs, we, too, can wither and dry up. Once ignored, it has a hard time getting back to where it was before. When distractions control our schedules we tend to let go of other things, including our faith.

We can keep healthy spiritually by placing our faith as a priority and giving it consistent attention. Don't let the distractions of life allow your faith to take a back seat. Nourish it with worship, Bible study, prayer and Sunday school classes. That only happens if faith is a priority.

We had to re-seed that patch of dirt, and we are committed to not letting it dry up again. Don't let your faith hit a dry spell. Make church a priority that never lets other commitments get in the way. Nourish it frequently, *especially* during times of stress when you need it the most.

Question: How can you keep from being distracted in exercising your faith in times of busyness and stress?

Scripture: *Blessed is the man who perseveres under trial, because when he has stood the test, he will receive the crown of life that God has promised to those who love him (James 1:12).*

Prayer: We pray we won't let down when times are tough. Those are the times when we need you the most. We pray we will always continue to nourish our faith, in good times and in bad. Amen.

Bruce Boyer

Topic: Reality

Soarin'

Disney World is one of our country's most popular tourist attractions. One of the newer Epcot Theme Park rides is called

"Soarin'." Riders are buckled onto a hang glider seat attached to a large metal frame. The lights dim and you shove off a cliff to begin your experience. You better not have a fear of heights as it takes you on the ride of a lifetime. The ride lifts you soaring high above the clouds, over California mountain ranges, and gliding above the Golden Gate Bridge. Then, it plunges down so close to the surface of a river you instinctively pick up your feet to avoid a splash down. Water gently sprays on your face. Spectacular video photography high altitude winds, and upward and downward motions of your hang glider, accompanied by a majestic musical score in surround sound audio, make it feel real. What an experience!

Once you land, the lights come on and you realize you haven't gone anywhere. What seemed real was an enhanced video production with effects to create the sensation of flying. Instead of sharing the sky with a pair of Air Force jets and hot air balloons, you realize you were only about 10 feet off the ground. It was wonderful and breath-taking, but it wasn't reality.

We experience many illusions in our lives. Enticing opportunities tempt us with our desire for fame, fortune, or the easy life. Satan does his best to make the temptations look good, but reality sets in when we recognize it is all "show." Satan tries to divert us from our godly path and baits us into thinking his proposition is better. After all, Satan offered Jesus all the kingdoms in the world in exchange for bowing down to worship the devil. Just one little knee bend and the world would belong to Jesus. Jesus didn't take the bait, nor should we.

Make no mistake about it; "Soarin'" was one of my favorite Disney experiences. It was fantasy but it looked and felt very real. The reality is Jesus Christ is Lord and Savior, and certainly not a simulation. I can enjoy the beauty of God's creation because I know the creator. He is God who helps separate reality from temptation and fantasy. Life is not all beautiful scenery and relaxing music. It has its share of real issues to face. God can take us soaring above the challenges we face if we trust and worship Him. That is reality.

Scripture: *Then Jesus was led up by the Spirit into the wilderness to be tempted by the devil...Again, the devil took Him up on an exceedingly high mountain, and showed Him all the kingdoms of the world and their glory. And he said to Him, "All these things I will give You if You will fall down and worship me." Then Jesus said to him, "Away with you, Satan! For it is written, 'You shall worship the LORD your God, and Him only you shall serve.'" (Matthew 4:1, 8-10).*

Question: How do you recognize and resist Satan's temptations?

Prayer: Help us to resist the devil's attempts to lure us into sin by making it look attractive and harmless. Satan wants nothing more than for us to turn our back on You, Lord. Let us stay strong in the faith. You are our reality. Amen.

Bruce Boyer

Topic: Right and Wrong

We Don't Make the Rules

Several years ago a featured Monday Night Football game matched the home team Carolina Panthers against the always powerful New England Patriots. The game came down to the final play. With the Panthers precariously clinging to a four-point lead, the New England Patriots were driv-

Ten Commandment Tablets

ing downfield. Patriot quarterback Tom Brady threw a pass into the end zone as the game clock reached zero. A receiver in the back of the end zone was the intended target but he was literally bear-hugged by a Panther defender. The pass was intercepted in the front of the end zone, well short of the intended receiver. Panther fans started to celebrate the game winning interception while Patriot fans started their own celebration when a yellow penalty flag came into the picture. The referees briefly huddled and then it was announced that it was not pass interference. The flag was picked up. The game was over.

Following the game, a referee supervisor was interviewed to give an interpretation of the rules in this situation. To the surprise of many, he supported the decision to pick up the penalty flag, reciting

80

and interpreting the actual rule that the ball was uncatchable. Even though it seemed logical a penalty should be called, the rules stated otherwise. For days, broadcasters still expressed their opinion the play was incorrectly called. It is human nature to cling to what we think it should be, even when fully explained by the experts.

Mankind has continually tried to write the rules of life to suit their own desires. It is our way of rationalizing to get what we want. We continue to think that right should change with the times. We want to bring God into the 21st century as if we were in charge and God needed updating. While we use disposable paper and fragile electronic media to communicate, God etches His rules in stone – the Ten Commandments. They don't change over time, even though we may want to bend them to suit our desires.

Seek out God's answers to your questions about what is right and wrong, and then accept His direction.

Scripture: *All your words are true; all your righteous laws are eternal (Psalm 119:160).*

Question: We often are tempted to change the rules to suit our needs. Or, we may feel that God's commandments are outdated. How do you hold true to God's commandments in today's world?

Prayer: It is easy to want our own way which is based on popular opinion rather than biblical truths. Lord, help us to understand and accept your commandments are eternal.

Bruce Boyer

Topic: Role Model

Becoming Like Our Parents?

My dad is a hardworking man. During his entire life I can only remember him missing work one time, with a three-day bout of flu. He persevered through colds and minor health issues and made his way to work, every day. We lived in a northern climate that received major snowfalls each year, but he never let that stop him from going where he wanted. He was always willing to help other people. He held open doors for people, and he always stayed after events to put away the chairs. What a great example of a servant leader!

Richard P. Boyer, Jr., my dad

When I look at my wife I see lots of her mother in her. Both were teachers by profession, and both took an interest in their students achieving outside the classroom as well as academically. Both were the kind of teachers to lead school trips and do the extra things that enhanced the learning experience. Both were students themselves – students of faith. Both joined service organizations. Both liked to play cards. Family was important in their lives. Both could be characterized as kind, loving people.

In Paul's letter to the Ephesians he says in chapter 5, *"Be imitators of God, therefore, as dearly loved children and live a life of love, just as Christ loved us...* (Ephesians 5:1-2). This verse asks us to imitate God, which is a tall order. God is forgiving, and so should we. The sacrificial way Jesus expressed his love for us is not only the means of salvation, but also an example of the way we are to live for the sake of others.

As we mature in life, and in our faith, let us strive to be in the image of our heavenly Father. *So God created man in his own image, in the image of God he created him; male and female he created them. (Genesis 1:27).* Just as our parents were good examples for us, God is the perfect example. Let us seek to be like our heavenly Father in all we do.

Question: In what ways do you model your heavenly Father?

Scripture: *How great is the love the Father has lavished on us, that we should be called children of God! And that is what we are! (1 John 3:1).*

Prayer: Heavenly Father, we want to be like You, loving others and living according to Your Word. We pray we can be more like You each day, serving as excellent examples of faith to our children.

Bruce Boyer

Topic: Sacrifice

Joy Ride

I read a short story about a man who saw the car of his dreams parked on the side of the road. The keys were in the ignition of the sporty convertible. Opportunity got the best of him. He jumped into the car, revved up the engine, and took it out for a spin around the block. He was so energized by the power he felt that, instead of guiding it back into its parking place, he turned onto the interstate and floored it. The exit was just two miles ahead. Everything was great until he saw the flashing blue lights of the patrol car. Busted, and certainly guilty of multiple sins.

When he made his court appearance, the situation took a major twist. As soon as the man confessed to the uninvited joy ride, the judge took off his robe, opened his wallet to pay the man's fine, and insisted on taking the man's warranted punishment. Then the judge looked the man in the eye and said, "I love you."

Jesus did the same for us. Totally innocent of any sin, Jesus substituted himself for each of us. He paid the price and accepted the punishment we deserved. He died a horrific death on the cross so that you and I could live. He does this because of His love for you and me.

How would you feel if a judge paid the fine and took the punishment you deserved? You probably would leave the courtroom awestruck that anyone would do that for you. You probably would be willing to do anything in return for the judge. Jesus did even more for you.

Question: Do you take it for granted or are you equally blown away by Jesus' sacrifice for you? What would you be willing to do for Jesus?

Scripture: *While we were unable to help ourselves, at the right time, Christ died for us, although we were living against God … God shows his great love for us in this way: Christ died for us while we were still sinners (Romans 5:6,8).*

Prayer: Lord, we thank You for Your love, and because of Your love for us, Your supreme sacrifice. We pray that Your sacrifice will make a difference in our lives.

Bruce Boyer

Topic: Serving Those in Need

Perspective

Many people will remember the winter of 2014. Locally, school was cancelled for nine days and many other days had either an early dismissal or delayed start. Facebook posts and national news showed far worse conditions in other parts of the country, particularly the Northeast and Midwest. Unrelenting winter storms seemed to come wave after wave all across the nation.

After enduring such a horrendous winter I was surprised to read a news article describing this as the 5th *warmest* winter in recorded history. No way. Did the *Mission Impossible* team substitute a video feed that fooled us into thinking we were experiencing a blizzard instead of balmy weather? And what about national news coverage showing snow drifts and multi-car vehicle accidents because of icy and snowy roads? Was all the

86

snow and ice just a mirage? It certainly wasn't short-sleeved, spring-like weather I would have anticipated in the 5th warmest winter in history.

There is a saying that "perception is reality," which means what you see is what you perceive as real. It is a pretty narrow-minded perspective, but people think what they see in front of them is how it is everywhere. There are sections of town we avoid because they seem dangerous or unsightly to us. We go about our daily lives acting as if these areas don't exist. The same goes for issues in our community. We tend to ignore what we don't see, in an "out of sight, out of mind" philosophy. Through our rose-colored glasses everything is great, which allows us to turn a blind eye to reality.

Churches do a good job of identifying areas where we can help, locally, regionally and globally. Mission trips and service opportunities physically place us in those areas of need, where we can see things as they *really* are. We are serving God when we serve the needy. Jesus said, *I tell you the truth, whatever you did for one of the least of these brothers of mine, you did for me* (Matthew 25:40).

Yes, it is a fact this winter was the 5th warmest ever. You had to look outside North America to understand that. Worldwide, it *was* a warm winter. The same is true of serving God by serving others; we need to look beyond our living room window to the opportunities to serve others in need, locally, regionally and globally.

The Great Commission tells us to spread God's Word to the world. We do that through sharing God's promises, but also by sharing His love through service to others in need.   Actions speak louder than words as we put faith into action. *He said to them, "Go into all the world and preach the good news to all creation"* (*Mark 16:15*). "All the world" broadens our perspective.

Question: What efforts have you made to find service opportunities in your community and in the world beyond?

Bruce Boyer

Prayer: It is easy to be near-sighted and ignore the needs of people outside our field of vision. Help us to become aware and reach out to serve people elsewhere.

Topic: Serving Others

Bringing a Smile to God's Face

Our community enjoys a series of concerts on the Town Hall lawn over the summer. There typically is a headliner group but also opening songs by an up-and-coming singer from the community. The opening act on one particular night was Annaelise Arnold, a talented high school fresh-man singer. Annaelise has sung numerous times at community concerts, the national anthem at professional baseball games and at other civic club events.

Annaelise Arnold performing at Music at Twilight concert with her mom in the background

If you look closely in the background of the photo below, you can see the reaction of her mom watching her daughter on stage. The mom is grinning from ear to ear.

God smiles lovingly at us when we do things to make Him happy on the stage of life. Just like parents are heavily invested in their children, God has invested a great deal in us. He has lovingly provided us skills and opportunities to serve, and patiently waited for us to use them. When we utilize those skills and show our servant's heart, it has to be satisfying to God.

The picture captured the mom's genuine sense of appreciation for what her daughter has become, using the God-given gift of musical talent. You can just see on the Mom's face the thought, "That's my daughter. And she is doing fantastic!" God was thinking the same thing with His son, Jesus Christ. *You are my Son, whom I love; with you I am well pleased.*

As parents, we so much want our children to succeed. When they do, it brings joy to a parent's heart. Serve God and you will bring a smile and joy to your heavenly Father. He will be talking about you when He says, "That's my boy" or "that's my girl."

Question: What God-given skills can you use to serve others?

Prayer: We thank you Lord for the many skills you have given us and the heart to use them to serve others. We pray that our efforts will be pleasing to you. Amen.

Topic: Sharing the Faith

And What About the Next Generation?

Recently I enjoyed a theatrical production depicting the life and music of Patsy Cline. The vast majority of the sold-out audience were seniors over the age of 60 -- people who grew up listening to

Country music star Patsy Cline

Patsy Cline, the country music star of the late 1950's and early 60's. Many of the seniors came into the theatre with walkers and some in wheel chairs. They came to relive the memories of a beloved star whose musical career abruptly ended in an airplane crash in 1963. It was a brief career but one that transformed country music into becoming popular on the radio and at New York City venues such as Carnegie Hall.

There is a parallel with the ministry of Jesus Christ. The actual time of Jesus Christ's adult ministry was only three years before being cut short in the prime of his life. Yet, his influence and teachings remain with us to this day, thanks to the efforts of generations before us.

Bruce Boyer

Driving home from the theatre, the question struck me: once Patsy Cline fans pass on, will her music have any relevance for future generations? No one will have actually experienced her music first-hand. We have only recordings and a few black and white films of this transformational performer. Even though her music changed the industry, it has already been replaced by the music of this generation. Twenty years from now when all of the Patsy Cline generation is gone, will anyone still know of her music?

Some of the same questions can be asked when we think of passing on the faith to future generations. Have we done all we could to ensure the candle of faith is strong in those younger than us? The words of the Bible, inspired by God, are written for all generations to read. Yet, we have to encourage others to read and embrace the lessons of Jesus Christ. Don't let the future sanctuaries of our churches be sparsely filled because no one inspired the next generation in their faith.

Let us actively and enthusiastically share our faith with those who follow us.

Question: How can you help keep the faith alive in the next generation?

Scripture: *It is written: "I believed, therefore I have spoken." With that same spirit of faith, we also believe and therefore speak (2 Corinthians 4:13).*

Prayer: Dear Lord, help us to fulfill our responsibility to keep the faith alive in the next generation.

Topic: Sharing the Faith

What Would You Take?

It is fun to play situation games: If your house was burning down and you could only take one thing out of the house, what would it be? If you were shipwrecked on a desert island and could choose to have only one item from the ship, what would it be? If you were lost in the woods ... The list of scenarios is as extensive as your imagination. Many are survival scenarios, trying to determine what will help you the most in a life-or-death scenario.

We may never have our house burn down or be shipwrecked on a deserted island, but there will come a time when we all pass from this world. At that time there are no material things we take with us. Regardless of the wealth you have amassed on this earth, none of it goes with you. Neither does your favorite car nor your beautifully decorated home. The vacation house, the boat -- you leave them all behind. The only thing you can take with you is ... (drum roll please) ... other people you have brought to faith.

Bruce Boyer

That is such a stark realization it should have some impact on our priorities in life. While we may seek the good life, what is lasting is the impact we have on others. We should seek to take as many people with us as we can.

When we compare the worth of people vs. objects we have acquired over our lifetime, people win every time. Knowing this, our goal should be to plant seeds that nurture other people in their faith. If we wish the people in our daily lives to be part of our eternal lives in heaven, our goal should be for them to accept Jesus Christ as their Lord and Savior. *If you confess with your mouth, "Jesus is Lord," and believe in your heart that God raised him from the dead, you will be saved (Romans 10:9).*

The Bible is clear on what it takes to get to heaven: faith that Jesus is Lord. Make God your priority and encourage others to be of faith. The result is a reunion of family and friends, together forever. It is a matter of life or death.

Scripture: *Our citizenship is in heaven. And we eagerly await a Savior from there, the Lord Jesus Christ (Philippians 3:20).*

Question: Are you making the effort to share your faith with others, encouraging them to be strong in their faith?

Prayer: We thank You for the opportunity to share our faith with others, Lord, in hopes those we touch will join us in heaven.

Topic: Sharing Your Faith

Returning the Favor

One of my favorite television commercials shows a beaver cross-ing the road carrying a tree limb in his mouth. An approaching car swerves to avoid hitting the beaver, saving its life. With a little humor, both beaver and driver salute each other. The tire commercial's next scene shows the same driver piloting his ve-hicle through a torrential rain-storm. As the car approach-es a bridge, a large tree limb suddenly falls across the road, causing the driver to make

an emergency stop. At that very moment, the bridge is swept away by a raging river. As the car comes to a stop, the driver looks up to see the same beaver by the side of the road. The beaver had cut down a tree with his teeth, causing it to fall in the vehicle's path. The actions of the beaver save the driver from a certain death as the bridge is washed away. Again, there is a celebratory gesture. The beaver had returned the life-saving favor.

Bruce Boyer

This story has a feel-good quality about it. A man saves the life of another creature of God. The beaver returns the favor, saving the driver from plunging into the river below, as the bridge collapses.

Someone in your life provided the encouragement that led you to faith. Perhaps it was a parent, friend, co-worker or another adult. We know that if you aren't a person of faith, the end will be a death our sins deserve. Yet, we will be saved because of our belief in Jesus Christ. The person who encouraged you, boldly "went out on a limb" to guide you in a new direction.

But, the story doesn't end there. There was a second scene in the tire commercial, as there often is in real life. As a saved member of God's family, *we* have the opportunity to help someone else come to faith.

Sometimes it takes boldness to "go out on a limb." Sharing the Gospel may not be in our comfort zone. We can, however, use whatever skills God gave us to reach out to others. The Holy Spirit gives you the power to make a difference. Who knows – our actions may come just as the person's life is about to collapse.

Someone helped you in your faith. Boldly return the favor by helping someone else.

But you will receive power when the Holy Spirit comes on you; and you will be my witnesses in Jerusalem, and in all Judea and Samaria, and to the ends of the earth (Acts 1:8).

Questions: If you know someone who is on the wrong road in life, are you willing to try to guide them? How can you serve as a warning of impending doom?

Prayer: Heavenly Father. Give us the courage to boldly step out in faith to help others strengthen their faith so they, too, may enjoy eternal life with You. Amen.

Topic: Strength

The Source of Our Strength

Tim Tebow: God's Quarterback - He has led the Denver Broncos to one improbable victory after another, defying his critics and revealing the deep-seated anxieties in American society about the intertwining of religion and sports.

"Tebowmania" captured the imagination of the football world in 2011. Tim Tebow is no longer an NFL starting quarterback, but his legacy gives us a unique perspective on how God works in unconventional ways. After a successful collegiate career, a Heisman Trophy, and two national championships, Tebow began his pro career with the Denver Broncos.

Denver Broncos Quarterback Tim Tebow celebrates a touchdown

News media and football analysts doubted Tim's abilities, finding flaws in his throwing mechanics. Even before he played his first game, he was fodder for criticism that he would be a bust on the field. God had other plans.

Tim Tebow is a man of God, forthright in his faith, and always crediting the Lord for any successes. As a youngster and young adult he participated in his parents' missionary assignments. On the football field he wrote Bible references on his face. That made him a target for naysayers who doubted the power of faith to inspire success in professional sports. The news media didn't know how to deal with a player who put God ahead of self. They thought having a servant's heart was a sign of weakness, and Tim wouldn't cut it in the NFL. They were wrong!

Tim started his rookie season on the Broncos' bench. Denver had a slow start to the season and by mid-season the starting job was his. Given the chance to play, game after game, Tim Tebow found a way to rally the team to fourth quarter wins, elevating the Broncos from the cellar to a tie for first place. His late-game heroics bordered on the miraculous. Yet the media still questioned his abilities. In his own humble way Tim Tebow always gave credit to God and compliments to his teammates. His success was clearly not all "about him," but instead was "all about Him."

There are many Bible stories that show how people of Jesus' time would only conditionally believe if Jesus continued to perform miracles on demand. To them, Jesus had to prove himself again and again. It was all about the show and not the true message. The people of Jesus' day were waiting for Him to fail just once so they could deny God. But Jesus was perfect and He never failed. On the other hand, Tim Tebow was not perfect. A human being with a heart for God, the Lord allowed Tim to orchestrate improbable miracle wins, knowing Tim would faithfully give the credit to God. The man with flawed mechanics and limited abilities clearly drew his strength from God. *So do not fear, for I am with you; do not be dismayed, for I am your God. I will strengthen you and help you; I will uphold you with my righteous right hand (Isaiah 41:10).*

But, the Doubting Thomases wanted more miracles the following season. God wasn't about to give in to the insatiable desire for miracle after miracle. God made his point with Tim Tebow's rookie season, and Tim won souls for Christ. Continuing the string of miracles would only play into the hands of unbelievers who only want the show and not the message.

God works through our flaws. He provided Tim the strength
to accomplish much in His name. And He will do the same for
you and me. It takes the commitment of faith to tap into God's
power. Although Tebow didn't duplicate his miracle rookie season, he had already won people for Christ. The mission had been
accomplished.   There comes a time when people need to believe
and not just crave more miracles.

God does things in unconventional ways and with unconventional people to win souls. When we accomplish something
significant in spite of our flaws, we are further demonstrating
God's power. God isn't concerned with winning the Super Bowl.
Instead, His goal is for people to want to worship the God that
gives power to the faithful.   After all, it is not about us, but is
about praising the source of our strength. *In the same way, let your
light shine before men, that they may see your good deeds and praise your
Father in heaven (Matthew 5:16).*

Question: How can you use God-given abilities to be a witness
to God and to encourage others in the strengthening of their
faith?

Prayer: Lord, we have limited abilities but we know we can do
all things through you. Help us to inspire others in faith as they
see our commitment to ours. Amen.

Bruce Boyer

Kryptonite

Since 1933, Superman has been a popular fictional character featured in comics, television shows, and full-length films. Kids dream about being Superman because he represents good in the world.

He has superhuman powers, especially the ability to fly. The red and blue outfit is as American as apple pie. Superman seeks "truth, justice and the American way."

Superman came to earth from the imaginary planet Krypton. He lived his earthly life as Clark Kent, a newspaper reporter for the <u>Daily Planet</u>. Superman's extraordinary powers defeated evil villains time after time. His most conniving opponent was Lex Luthor, who discovered Superman lost all his powers when in the presence of kryptonite. Luthor relished the thought of defeating Superman, opening an unimpeded path to wreak havoc on the world. He continually tried to find ways to trick Superman into exposure to kryptonite.

The fictional Lex Luthor is like Satan in our real world. Satan wants to conquer the world for his own evil purposes. Satan hates good in the world and continually plots ways to destroy the faith of righteous people. Satan tries to trick us to exploit our weaknesses.

Lead protects Superman from Kryptonite, serving as a shield against its deadly force.

We have a shield, too. Our shield from Satan is the Word of God coupled with the strength of our faith. It takes both to combat the forces of evil. Faith without the Word of God cannot withstand constant attacks from Satan. The foundation of our faith is the written Word of God. Knowledge of the scriptures and God's wonderful promises is the rock, empowering us to withstand Satan's attacks. The Bible is our instruction book.

Satan is motivated by greed, hate and power. God's motivation is love, and He unlocks our path to heaven.

The more good deeds Superman does, the more fiercely he is challenged by Lex Luthor. The stronger our faith, the harder the devil will work to separate us from that faith. Even a person with superhuman strength doesn't make it with good deeds alone. It takes faith in a power much greater than our own abilities. We have access to that higher power through prayer, worship and the Bible. Let God be the shield protecting you in this real world.

Scripture: *God is our protection and our strength. He always helps in times of trouble … The Lord, All-Powerful is with us; the God of Jacob is our defenders (Psalm 46:1, 11).*

Question: In what ways do you recognize Satan's efforts to separate you from your loving God? How do you resist the evil temptations thrown in your path?

Prayer: Heavenly Father, we love You and know You love us. Give us the strength to resist the temptations of the devil so we may lead righteous lives.

Bruce Boyer

Updates Are Ready for Your Computer

My computer is constantly in need of software updates. It seems that every day a message pops up on my monitor saying "updates are ready for your computer." Software engineers are continually patching loopholes and glitches in the software to make the operating system work better and to protect me. Updates are essential to safeguard the computer from malicious hackers trying to steal important personal information that could lead to identity theft. Having the mindset that the computer was working just fine without updates is a recipe for disaster.

Anti-virus programs scan incoming messages and my hard drive, looking for viruses specifically written to destroy computers. Last week's anti-virus software is not sufficient to handle this week's viruses.

Sounds like a dangerous world to me!

Some of us are so diligent about protection that we set our computer to do it automatically, and notify us the work is done. There are simply too many updates to rely on our constant attention. We wake up in the morning to a computer message that confirms we have been protected.

What a changing world we live in. Computers could be rendered useless if we didn't constantly update what makes them work, and safeguard them from human-caused diseases. So, what about us? If we are being bombarded with threats, are we updating our faith to handle the new challenges to our lives?

Hall of Fame baseball player Yogi Berra said, "Yesterday's skills don't win today's games." So why is it that many of us try to live our lives on yesterday's spiritual knowledge? What we learned in confirmation class years ago isn't enough if we have since stopped learning. If the world is changing so rapidly, why do we stand pat with our own basic knowledge of God's Word? Do we update our knowledge daily with Bible reading? Do we regularly attend Bible study classes to help us increase our understanding and application of that knowledge in the changing world in which we live?

Updating our spiritual life is not as easy as updating a computer. We can set the computer to do it for us automatically, usually while we sleep. Updating our knowledge and understanding God's Word takes conscious effort yet is essential to handling today's issues and challenges. Satan is the ultimate malicious hacker, trying to ruin your life. He would like to steal your identity as a child of God. You need the constant reinforcement of new spiritual knowledge to fend off his attacks.

Scripture: *For wisdom will come into your heart, and knowledge will be pleasant to your soul; discretion will watch over you, understanding will guard you (Proverbs 2:10-11).*

Question: How do you increase your knowledge of God's Word and its application to your life today?

Prayer: We know, Lord, it is important to continually increase our spiritual knowledge. We pray we will not rely on limited, outdated knowledge to deal with today's problems. Amen.

104

Topic: Seasonal/Easter

Roller Coaster Ride

Most of us have ridden a roller coaster at least once in our lives.

The thrill ride features sharp turns, and some even take you upside down. Invariably, roller coasters have at least one slow, steady climb to the highest point on the ride. Even though the car is ascending slowly, your heart is pounding already, anticipating what is to come. When you reach the top, you are looking practically straight down, knowing the bottom is getting ready to drop out as you start your screaming descent

To the casual observer, Holy Week between Palm Sunday and Easter was a roller coaster ride for Jesus. On Palm Sunday Jesus rode into Jerusalem on the back of a donkey, crowds wildly cheering. The crowd was aware of his many miracles performed in recent days.

So, they cheered on their King – but for the wrong reasons. Their expectation was for Jesus to use his powers to save them from the Roman rulers.

Just four days later Jesus would gather with his disciples in the Upper Room, washing their feet as a sign of humility and love. He would also serve the bread and wine of the Last Supper. Immediately following the meal, things quickly unraveled. Judas betrayed him to the Roman soldiers and his closest disciple, Peter, denied him not once but three times. Fearing for their own lives, the other disciples fled to hiding places. Disaster struck the next day. Knowing of Jesus' innocence, Pontius Pilate asked the crowds what he should do with Jesus. Some of the same people who cheered his entrance into Jerusalem a few days prior now said to "Crucify him." Shrouded in mid-day darkness, Jesus was nailed to a cross. He was mocked, jeered, and ridiculed. Jesus himself uttered the words, *It is finished (John 19:30)*. The ground trembled as Jesus took His last breath. His lifeless body was placed in a tomb, sealed by a heavy stone. Followers mourned his passing. What a disappointing turn of events. Just a few days after the most triumphal time, it all seemed lost.

And then, on Easter Sunday morning, the events of the day soared higher than the most spectacular roller coaster could ever reach. Jesus rose from the dead. He came out of the tomb even before the angels rolled the stone away. The empty tomb created wonder and anticipation. Jesus revealed himself to Mary, several women, and eventually the disciples. *He has risen, just as He said he would, said the angel (Matthew 28:6)*. Jesus had conquered death – not just for himself, but for all believers, too. What a week of ups and downs.

To the observers it was a roller coaster of a week, but not to Jesus. Jesus anticipated all that was to happen. As humans, we ride the wave of emotions. We are "up" when things are going well, and sink into despair when things fall apart. We react this way because we don't let our faith mediate the ups and downs of life. Jesus knew all along what was happening and the purpose behind each of the events of Holy Week. It was all part of the plan.

Jesus' motivation was love for us and his purpose was to save people from their sins.

What does this mean for how we handle the ups and downs of life? Jesus promised to be with us all the time, through the twists and turns of life. Knowing Jesus' love for us is how we overcome the lows and stay grounded in the highs of life. You know that God will carry you over or through the issues you face. With Jesus next to you, life's roller coaster ride is predictable and manageable. He takes away your fears, if you let him. You can be assured the ending will be the victory of eternal life. You know that Jesus loves you no matter what issues you face. And because you follow Jesus, you can count on Him. Just stay buckled in your seat of faith and Jesus will lead you to eternal life. Jesus took that ride for you, and for me.

Question: When you face difficulties, how do you place your trust in Jesus to carry you through?

Scripture: *When I am afraid, I will trust you. I praise God for his word. I trust God, so I am not afraid. What can human beings do to me? (Psalm 56:3-4).*

Prayer: Lord, life has its ups and downs, but You carry us through the difficult times if we put our trust in You.

Bruce Boyer

Topic: Trust

From Pink Slip to Capitol Hill

A 2009 corporate downsizing put a spunky young financial planner out of a job. The nation-wide finan-cial recession was causing widespread unemploy-ment. An-chored by faith, Jen-ny Fulton concluded, "When one

JennyFulton (Miss Jenny's Pickles) meets Vice President Joe Biden

door closes, God opens another." With God's perfect timing the sermon series at her church centered on the theme, "If you want to walk on water you've got to get out of the boat," based on the John Ortberg book of the same title.

To depict the theme, a canoe was placed on the altar. Pastor Keith Speaks talked about taking bold steps in a new direction, relying on God for strength during the storms of life. Jenny took the message to heart and explored a new career: a start-up pickle business. Using a favorite family recipe, she and her business partner, Ashlee Furr, prepared and canned pickles at a local YMCA kitchen. Thanks to their limitless energy, in just a few short years their pickles would be on the shelves of thousands of stores around the world.

The familiar Bible story of Peter getting out of the boat to walk on the water towards Jesus was the text for the sermon series. For Peter,

Canoe on the altar of Fountain of Life Lutheran Church, as part of the sermon series If You Want to Walk on Water You Have to Get out of the Boat

even in the presence of Jesus, it was not all clear sailing. Peter began to sink when he had a moment of doubt as strong winds picked up. Noticing Jesus; outstretched arms, Peter refocused his eyes on Christ. Immediately Peter rose back to the surface.

Jenny had her moments of doubt, too. There were times when the turbulence of the business world created fear and uncertainty. For Jenny, those were the times when she had to refocus her eyes on Jesus. Like Peter, she rose again to the surface. She took comfort in the thought that "God has brought me this far. He is not going to leave me now." It is time to stop and pray, and ask for Jesus' outstretched hand.

God reaches out his hand to you if you ask. Fix your eyes on Jesus and He will become the foundation of your success. Asking God to carry you through the storms of life isn't a one-time prayer. Invite Jesus to be the CEO of your life, with constant communication and trust in His leadership.

There is more to Jenny's story. God didn't rescue Jenny from unemployment just to sell a few pickles. God had a bigger plan. A short four years after the first jar of pickles, "Chief Pickle" Jenny Fulton had become a national spokesperson for small business. She has testified to the U.S. House of Representatives Subcommittee on Agriculture, Energy and Trade, encouraging our government to assist small business success. Jenny had become a dynamic business woman who inspired our nation's leaders and a motivational speaker around the country. God had transformed Jenny from a young financial planner to a successful business woman and spiritual leader. It all started with a big step out of the boat in the sanctuary of her church. She trusted a loving God who had stretched out His loving hand, saying come to me. God will help you accomplish your goals if you have faith.

Jenny did not bury the fruits of her successful business in a bank account or in a hole beside a cucumber patch. As a motivational speaker and author she frequently shares the secret of her God-given success. Peter was anything but silent sharing Jesus' teachings with the world. Jenny also has a message to tell others. "Keep your head up. You're not alone." To her, she succeeded because she was willing to step out of her comfort zone, trust a loving God, and then act on that trust. God grew not only the cucumbers but also the heart of Jenny and Ashlee. God knew Jenny would be a spokesperson that would inspire others. The chairman of the U.S. House committee affirmed Jenny's testimony with the comment, "I can see why you can sell pickles." Jenny can do much more than that. She can inspire others to trust God with their lives.

As one door closes, allow God to point to a new direction and step out of the boat. Trust that God will lead you from despair to success beyond your wildest dreams. *Jesus immediately reached out his hand and caught him, saying to him, 'You of little faith, why did you doubt?' (Matthew 14:31).*

Question: In what areas of your life do you need to step out of your comfort zone and trust God to lead you?

Prayer: Heavenly Father, give us the courage to ask You for help and trust You will lead us the right direction, if we follow You. Amen.

Topic: Wants vs. Needs

The Grocery Store Strategy

The scene is all too familiar. A parent with a small child is in the grocery store line near you. While the parent is busy trans-

ferring food from the cart to the check-out belt, the youngster's attention zeroes in on other things. The child knows he has approximately precious seconds to select a conveniently placed piece of candy or toy and plop it on the belt. Timing is every-thing. The item appears just before the cashier pushes the "total" button on the cash register. Put the item on the belt too early and the parent will have more time to react, knowing he or she has been manipulated by the child. The cashier patiently waits for parental approval. Even the slightest pause in this transaction sends the youngster into plan B. Depending on what strategy has the best chance of success, the youngster either lets out a piercing scream or puts on their best innocent look, ac-companied by a sorrowful voice, saying, "Pleeease." If extra per-suasion is needed, the youngster quickly adds the phrase, "Just this one time." Tears are added sometimes for more drama.

The parent has been set up by a skillful child who knows just what buttons to push, and when. If the decision is no, the parent has to decide how to decline gracefully in front of fellow grocery store shoppers. Frequently the polite parental response is, "You don't need that now" or "not today, honey." To that, plan C is bartering, saying he will pick up his room or do some other task he should have done in the first place.

If the child takes the ear-piercing scream approach, the parent is forced into a proportionate response, including anger and threats.

Generally, the child is asking for something he wants, not something he needs. Impulse items are strategically placed at the exact spot where parent, child, temptation, and money converge. If denied, the child sounds like he is either dying or being beaten cruelly.

We are not as dramatic in our requests to God, but we often attempt to make a want seem like a need? We may even barter with God, promising to do something we should have done in the first place **if** God grants this request. Also like the child, we barter only if we don't think we are going to get our request granted any other way. Do we really think we can manipulate God?

Our heavenly Father is a loving God who wants us to be fulfilled. Like a wise parent, God knows the difference between what we want and what we need. God can see into the future, so His judgment is perfect. Trust in God's judgment and take comfort knowing He hears your prayers and answers them in His own perfect timing.

We have heard the "ask and you will receive" paraphrase from the Bible. That sounds too simple, and it is. In your prayers, seek God's will and not your own. His will is for you to prosper if you are doing things for God and not just yourself. Jesus said, *"Until now you have not asked for anything in my name. Ask and you will receive, and your joy will be complete"* (John 16:24).

Question: Do your prayers seek wants or needs?

Prayer: Lord, help us to be satisfied with the many blessings You give us, and to understand You provide what we need.

Bruce Boyer

Peace That Surpasses All Understanding

Watching the local or national news can be discouraging. Thanks to satellite transmissions we can witness tragic events around the world in real time. Natural disasters anywhere in the world are touted as evidence of global warming and are tied into unusual stateside weather patterns. When Wall Street stock prices drop, the media warns of us of an impending financial crisis. Closer to home, reports of plant closings make us  all fear for our ability to support our families. We are bombarded constantly by news of the instability of the Social Security system and rising health care costs. There is no end in sight to the bad news, most of which is beyond our control anyway.

How do you handle the constant bad news each day? Perhaps a better question is, will worrying do any good? *Therefore I tell you, do not worry about your life, what you will eat or drink; or about your body, what you will wear. Is not life more than food, and the body more than clothes? Look at the birds of the air; they do not sow or reap or store away in barns, and yet your heavenly Father feeds them. Are you not much more valuable than they? Can any one of you by worrying add a single hour to your life? (Matthew 6:25-27).*

The Bible provides a solution to worry: *Give all your worries and cares to God, for he cares about you (1 Peter 5:7).*

You may say, "So what. What is God going to do about these issues?" God can prepare you for what you are facing. First, tell God what is troubling you. *Do not be anxious about anything, but in every situation, by prayer and petition, with thanksgiving, present your requests to God (Philippians 4:6).* The result of your faith is: *And the peace of God, which transcends all understanding, will guard your hearts and your minds in Christ Jesus (Philippians 4:7).*

Even though we are programmed to ask why and how things happen, we don't need to question God's power or ability to make things right. The full dimensions of God's love and care are beyond human comprehension. His power gives us peace. That should be enough for us to let it go. In many of Christ's healing miracles Jesus said, *your faith has healed you (Matthew 9:22).* It just took an expression of faith.

Why make things more complicated? Make your requests to a loving God and then let Him take your burdens from you. Don't hold onto them at the same time you are trying to give them to God. That tug-of-war is not letting go. Trust God and rest in the assurance of his peace. He will either take you through the problems you face or take you above them.

Live in faith and in peace. Leave the rest up to God.

Question: How can you let go of your problems and have faith in the Creator to allow Him to handle them?

Prayer: Heavenly Father, our world is full of problems that cause us to worry. We ask You to help us let go and experience the peace that passes all understanding.

Bruce Boyer

Topic: Worship

Going Through the Motions

As the airplane rolls back from the gate, the flight attendant begins their required safety announcements. After welcoming you to the airline, the attendant tells you the destination – and then it all becomes a blur. You are tuned in only long enough to ensure you are on the right plane and immediately go back to "Never Never Land." You may appear to be watching the visual demonstrations of safety equipment but your mind is elsewhere. You have heard all this before, so why bother?

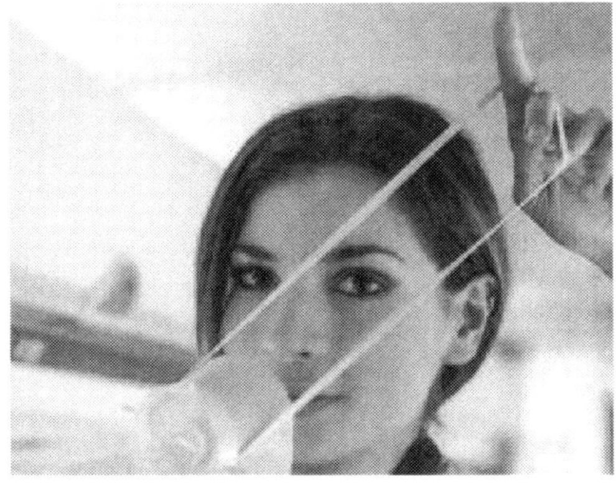

Is your Sunday morning also the same routine? Are you content to know the scheduled destination, but then tune out the rest? Have you heard it all before, so you can direct your attention to more pressing matters – the afternoon's activities, lunch, or reviewing the details of an unpleasant conversation from yesterday? You hear a couple of words of the familiar scripture reading and conclude you have heard it all before. Has your mind shifted into a "sit back, relax, and enjoy the flight" mode? Are you counting on auto pilot to get to that desired heavenly destination without attention and active involvement?

You aren't an uninvolved passenger in this trip of a lifetime. In order to reach the desired heavenly destination you need to be intimately involved in determining the flight plan, including how to fly through the storms of life. You may need God's safety equipment after all. Each time you hear the readings or the particular sermon, you may have new revelations – if you pay attention.

I have heard a saying that "If God is your co-pilot, you need to switch seats." There is truth to that statement. Allow God to be at the controls, with you in the cockpit, actively involved in your learning and confirming your direction.

Don't let the messages of the Sunday morning readings, inspirational music, and sermon fall on deaf ears while your mind is elsewhere. Your mere presence in church doesn't cut it. You need to be actively involved to prepare for the next step of your life. A safe landing depends on it.

The more difficult the week ahead, the more important is the spiritual renewal from the service you attend, physically and mentally.

Be ready when the call comes to board your flight. It may be the final call.

Scripture: *The time is coming when the true worshippers will worship the Father in spirit and truth, and that time is here already. You see, the Father too is actively seeking such people to worship him. God is spirit, and those who worship him must worship in spirit and truth (John 4:23-24).*

Question: What can you do to stay mentally involved in worship?

Prayer: It is easy to slip into auto-pilot, not paying attention in worship or to opportunities to increase our knowledge of You. Help us to make growing our faith a top priority in our lives.

Bruce Boyer

Topical Bible Reference Guide

What Does a Loving God Say About What You Face in Daily Life?

Adversity

- *Be strong and take heart, all you who hope in the Lord (Psalm 31:24).*

- *When I am afraid, I will trust in you, in God, whose word I praise, in God I trust; I will not be afraid (Psalm 56:3).*

Blessings

- *Every good and perfect gift is from above, coming down from the Father of the heavenly lights, who does not change like shifting shadows (James 1:17).*

- *The same Lord is the Lord of all and gives many blessings to all who trust in Him, as the Scripture says, "Anyone who calls on the Lord will be saved" (Romans 10:12-13).*

- *Praise be to the God and Father of our Lord Jesus Christ. In Christ, God has given us every spiritual blessing in the heavenly world. That is, in Christ, he chose us before the world was made so that we would be His holy people – people without blame before him (Ephesians 1:3-4).*

Choices

- *There is a way that appears to be right, but in the end it leads to death (Proverbs 14:12).*

- *Whether you turn to the right or to the left, your ears will hear a voice behind you, saying, "This is the way; walk in it" (Isaiah 30:21).*

- *Trust in the LORD with all your heart and do not lean on your own understanding. In all your ways acknowledge Him, and He will make your paths straight. Do not be wise in your own eyes; Fear the LORD and turn away from evil (Proverbs 3:5-7).*

- *Therefore, if anyone is in Christ, the new creation has come: The old has gone, the new is here! (2 Corinthians 5:17).*

Commitment

- *Love the LORD your God with all your heart and with all your soul and with all your strength (Deuteronomy 6:5).*

- *Commit to the LORD whatever you do, and he will establish your plans (Proverbs 16:3).*

Control

- *And we know that in all things God works for the good of those who love him, who have been called according to his purpose (Romans 8:28).*

- *Have I not commanded you? Be strong and courageous. Do not be afraid; do not be discouraged, for the LORD your God will be with you wherever you go (Joshua 1:9).*

- *Therefore do not worry about tomorrow, for tomorrow will worry about itself. Each day has enough trouble of its own (Matthew 6:34).*

- *For dominion belongs to the LORD and he rules over the nations (Psalms 22:28).*

Decisions

- *This is what the Lord says: "Stand at the crossroads and look; ask for the ancient paths, ask where the good way is, and walk in it and you will find rest for your souls" (Jeremiah 6:16).*

- *If any of you lacks wisdom, he should ask God, who gives generously to all without finding fault, and it will be given to him (James 1:5).*

- *"Call to me and I will answer you and tell you great and unsearchable things you do not know," says the Lord Jeremiah 33:3).*

- *Jesus said, "I will ask the Father, and He will give you another Counselor to be with you forever – the Spirit of truth. The world cannot accept Him, because it neither sees Him nor knows Him. But you know Him, for He lives with you and will be in you" John 14:16-17).*

- *This is what the Lord Almighty says: "Give careful thought to your ways" (Haggai 1:5).*

Faith

- *Since we have been justified through faith, we have peace with God through our Lord Jesus Christ (Romans 5:1).*

- *Jesus said, "I tell you the truth, if you have faith as small as a mustard seed, you can say to this mountain, 'Move from here to there' and it will move. Nothing will be impossible for you" (Matthew 17:20).*

- *Through Christ you believe in God, who raised Him from the dead and glorified Him, and so your faith and hope are in God (1 Peter 1:21).*

Fear

- *Joshua said to them, "Do not be afraid; do not be discouraged. Be strong and courageous. This is what the LORD will do to all the enemies you are going to fight" (Joshua 10:25).*

- *But the LORD said to him, "Peace! Do not be afraid. You are not going to die" (Judges 6:23).*

- *So do not fear, for I am with you; do not be dismayed, for I am your God. I will strengthen you and help you; I will uphold you with my righteous right hand (Isaiah 41:10).*

- *But Jesus came and touched them. "Get up," he said. "Don't be afraid" (Matthew 17:7).*

- *One night the Lord spoke to Paul in a vision: "Do not be afraid; keep on speaking, do not be silent" (Luke 18:9).*

Forgiveness

- *Peter replied, "Repent and be baptized, every one of you, in the name of Jesus Christ for the forgiveness of your sins. And you will receive the gift of the Holy Spirit" (Acts 2:38).*

- *In Jesus we have redemption through his blood, the forgiveness of sins, in accordance with the riches of God's grace (Ephesians 1:7).*

- *Jesus said, "If you forgive men when they sin against you, your heavenly Father will also forgive you (Matthew 6:14).*

Friendship

- *Be devoted to one another in brotherly love. Honor one another above yourselves (Romans 12:10.*

- *Jesus said, "Greater love has no one than this, that he lay down his life for his friends" (John 15:13).*

- *Two are better than one, because they have a good return for their work; if one falls down, his friend can help him up. But pity the man who falls and has no one to help him up! (Ecclesiastes 4:9-10).*

- *As iron sharpens iron, so one man sharpens another (Proverbs 27:17).*

Grace

- *From the fullness of his grace we have all received one blessing after another (John 1:16).*

- *It is by grace you have been saved, through faith – and this not from yourselves, it is the gift of God – not by works, so that no one can boast. For we are God's workmanship, created in Christ Jesus to do good works, which God prepared in advance for us to do (Ephesians 2:8-10).*

Grounded in Faith

- *So that Christ may dwell in your hearts through faith. And I pray that you, being rooted and established in love (Ephesians 3:17).*

- *Rooted and built up in him, strengthened in the faith as you were taught, and overflowing with thankfulness (Colossians 2:7).*

- *If you continue in your faith, established and firm, and do not move from the hope held out in the gospel. This is the gospel that you heard and that has been proclaimed to every creature under heaven, and of which I, Paul, have become a servant (Colossians 1:23).*

Heaven

- *God will wipe every tear from their eyes. There will be no more death or mourning or crying or pain, for the old order of things has passed away (Revelation 21:4).*

- *Our citizenship is in heaven. And we eagerly await a Savior from there, the Lord Jesus Christ (Philippians 3:20).*

Hope

- *This I call to mind and therefore I have hope: because of the Lord's great love we are not consumed, for his compassions never fail (Lamentations 3:21-22).*

- *The Lord's love never ends; his mercies never stop. They are new every morning; Lord, your loyalty is great. I say to myself, "The Lord is mine, so I hope in Him." The Lord is good to those who hope in Him, to those who seek Him (Lamentations 3:22-25).*

- *If God is with us, no one can defeat us. He did not spare His own Son but gave Him for us all. So with Jesus, God will surely give us all things. Who can accuse the people God has chosen? No one, because God is the One who makes them right (Romans 8:31-33).*

Image of God

- *Be perfect, therefore, as your heavenly Father is perfect (Matthew 5:48).*

- *And to put on the new self, created to be like God in true righteousness and holiness (Ephesians 4:24).*

- *Does he who fashioned the ear not hear? Does he who formed the eye not see? (Psalms 94:9).*

Joy

- *You make me glad by your deeds, O Lord; I sing for joy at the works of your hands (Psalm 92:4).*

- *Though you have not seen him, you love Him; and even though you do not see Him now, you believe in Him and are filled with an inexpressible and glorious joy, for you are receiving the goal of your faith, the salvation of your souls (1 Peter 1:8-9).*

- *Consider it pure joy, my brothers, whenever you face trials of many kinds, because you know that the testing of your faith develops perseverance (James 1:2-3).*

Love

- *Jesus said, "Whoever has my commands and obeys them, he is the one who loves me. He who loves me will be loved by my Father, and I too will love him and show myself to Him" (John 14:21).*

- *Anyone who does not love his brother, whom he has seen, cannot love God, whom he has not seen. And he has given us this command: Whoever loves God must also love his brother (1 John 4:20-21).*

- *We love because He first loved us (1 John 4:19).*

Bruce Boyer

- *Love each other deeply, because love covers over a multitude of sins (1 Peter 4:8).*

Patience

- *Wait for the Lord; be strong and take heart and wait for the Lord (Psalm 27:14).*

- *As for me, I watch in hope for the Lord, I wait for God my Savior; my God will hear me (Micah 7:7).*

- *A patient man has great understanding, but a quick-tempered man displays folly (Proverbs 14:29).*

Perseverance

- *Blessed is the man who perseveres under trial, because when he has stood the test, he will receive the crown of life that God has promised to those who love Him (James 1:12).*

- *Stand firm. Let nothing move you. Always give yourselves fully to the work of the Lord, because you know that your labor in the Lord is not in vain (1 Corinthians 15:58).*

- *To those who by persistence in doing good seek glory, honor and immortality, He will give eternal life (Romans 2:7).*

- *Let us not become weary in doing good, for at the proper time we will reap a harvest if we do not give up (Galatians 6:9).*

Prayer

- *Jesus said, "If you remain in me and my words remain in you, ask whatever you wish and it will be given you" (John 15:7).*

- *Pray in the Spirit on all occasions with all kinds of prayers and requests. With this in mind, be alert and always keep on praying for all the saints (Ephesians 6:18).*

Priority of Faith

- *God is fair; He will not forget the work you did and the love you showed for Him by helping His people. And He will remember that you are still helping them. We want each of you to go on with the same hard work all your lives so you will surely get what you hope for (Hebrews 6:10-11).*

- *But seek first his kingdom and his righteousness, and all these things will be given to you as well (Matthew 6:33).*

- *Do not conform to the pattern of this world, but be transformed by the renewing of your mind. Then you will be able to test and approve what God's will is—his good, pleasing and perfect will (Romans 12:2).*

- *For where your treasure is, there your heart will be also (Like 12:34).*

- *You shall have no other gods before me (Exodus 20:3).*

Right and Wrong

- *If anyone, then, knows the good they ought to do and doesn't do it, it is sin for them (Jams 4:17).*

- *Let everyone be subject to the governing authorities, for there is no authority except that which God has established. The authorities that exist have been established by God (Romans 13:1).*

- *And whatever you do, whether in word or deed, do it all in the name of the Lord Jesus, giving thanks to God the Father through him (Colossians 3:17).*

- *There is a way that appears to be right, but in the end it leads to death (Proverbs 14:12).*

Role Models

- *In the same way, let your light shine before others, that they may see your good deeds and glorify your Father in heaven (Matthew 5:16).*

- *Finally, brothers and sisters, whatever is true, whatever is noble, whatever is right, whatever is pure, whatever is lovely, whatever is admirable—if anything is excellent or praiseworthy—think about such things (Philippians 4:8).*

- *Then Jesus said to his disciples, "Whoever wants to be my disciple must deny themselves and take up their cross and follow me" (Matthew 16:24).*

- *Follow my example, as I follow the example of Christ (1 Corinthians 11:1).*

Sacrifice

- *And do not forget to do good and to share with others, for with such sacrifices God is pleased (Hebrews 13:16).*

- *For God so loved the world that he gave his one and only Son, that whoever believes in him shall not perish but have eternal life (John 3:16).*

- *Not looking to your own interests but each of you to the interests of the others (Philippians 2:4).*

Serving God By Serving Others

- *In all the work you are doing, work the best you can. Work as if you were doing it for the Lord, not for people. Remember that you will receive your reward from the Lord, which He promised to his people. You are serving the Lord Christ (Colossians 3:23-24).*

Sharing the Faith

- *That is, that you and I may be mutually encouraged by each other's faith (Romans 1:12).*

- *Therefore go and make disciples of all nations, baptizing them in the name of the Father and of the Son and of the Holy Spirit*

Stories of Faith from Everyday Life

(Matthew 28:19).

- *But in your hearts revere Christ as Lord. Always be prepared to give an answer to everyone who asks you to give the reason for the hope that you have. But do this with gentleness and respect (1 Peter 3:15).*

Strength

- *My flesh and my heart may fail, but God is the strength of my heart and my portion forever (Psalm 73:26).*

- *The Lord gives strength to the weary and increases the power of the weak (Isaiah 40:29).*

- *God is our refuge and strength, an ever-present help in trouble (Psalm 46:1).*

- *May God strengthen your hearts so that you will be blameless and holy in the presence of our God and Father when our Lord Jesus comes with all his holy ones (1 Thessalonians 3:13).*

Trust

- *It is better to take refuge in the Lord than to trust in man (Psalm 118:8).*

- *Jesus said, "Trust in God; trust also in me" (John 14:1).*

- *Blessed is the man who trusts in the Lord, whose confidence is in Him. He will be like a tree planted by the water that sends out its roots by the stream. It does not fear when heat comes; its leaves are always green. It has no worries in a year of drought and never fails to bear fruit (Jeremiah 17:7-8).*

Wants vs. Needs

- *And my God will meet all your needs according to the riches of his glory in Christ Jesus (Philippians 4:19).*

- *Therefore I tell you, do not worry about your life, what you will eat or drink; or about your body, what you will wear. Is not life more than food, and the body more than clothes? (Matthew 6:25).*

- *The Lord is my shepherd. I shall not want (Psalm 23:1).*

Worry

- *Jesus said, "Don't let your hearts be troubled. Trust in God, and trust in me" (John 14:1).*

- *You, Lord, give true peace to those who depend on you, because they trust you. So, trust the Lord always, because He is our Rock forever (Isaiah 26:3-4).*

- *Peace I leave with you; my peace I give you. I do not give to you as the world gives. Do not let your hearts be troubled and do not be afraid (John 14:27).*

- *Let the peace of Christ rule in your hearts, since as members of one body you were called to peace. And be thankful (Colossians 3:15).*

- *Come to me, all you who are weary and burdened, and I will give you rest. Take my yoke upon you and learn from me, for I am gentle and humble in heart, and you will find rest for your souls. For my yoke is easy and my burden is light (Matthew 11:28-30).*

Worship

- *Respect the Lord your God. You must worship Him and make your promises only in His name. Do not worship other gods as the people around you do, because the Lord your God is a jealous God (Deuteronomy 6:13-15).*

- *Say to God, "Your works are amazing! Because your power is great, your enemies fall before you. All the earth worships you and sings praises to you. They sing praises to your name" (Psalm 66:3-4).*

- *LORD, you are my God; I will exalt you and praise your name, for in perfect faithfulness you have done wonderful things, things planned long ago (Isaiah 25:1).*

- *Praise the LORD, my soul; all my inmost being, praise his holy name (Psalm 103:1).*

- *Give thanks to the LORD, for he is good; his love endures forever (1 Chronicles 16:34).*

Bruce Boyer

About The Author

There are no divinity degrees on the walls of our author, Bruce Boyer. God works through the common, ordinary man to be his hands on earth. I am as common and ordinary as they come. My background comes from a 34-year old YMCA professional career and 7 summers as a "Y " camp counselor. Founded in 1844 as a Bible study organization, the YMCA retains a Christian mission to this day. The third letter in its acronym stands for Christian. YMCA's that live up to their mission have

devotions at the beginnng of meetings, cabin devotions at camp, sports programs that begin with a pre-game prayer and character development lessons. The Y's Christian emphasis in the summer camp cabin was the begining of my devotional story telling.

In my adult life, I have been fortunate to be involved

in several national YMCA Christian empasis programs - Christian Leadership Conferences and the Rags & Leather programs. These programs encourage Christian principles to be included in all aspects of our lives.

The final 10 years of my professional career I served as president & CEO of the Kernersville Chamber of Commerce. One of my personal goals was to foster a wholesome, Christian community. It was a prefect setting to test the concept of seeing faith lessons in everyday life and not just in a church or Christian organization setting. We all have the opportunity to express our Christian faith in the greater secular community.

Being an active member in the leadership at my church, Fountain of Life Lutheran Church, is a foundation of more formal learning about the scriptures. Participation in Bible study is an important step to grow your faith.

The moment of truth of my faith was in 2002. My son had been exploring the remote Amazon rainforest of Brazil when he and a friend became lost for six days. God put into place all the elements for, literally, a last minute rescue. Dave and his companion had lost hope for their survival. That is precisely when God took over. God orchestrated a miracle rescue, and He did it for a purpose. Their rescue changed many lives, including my own. Always a person of my own personal faith, in thanks to God, I promised Him I would be more intentional in sharing my faith. In the years since I have written hundreds of real-life stories, accompanied with a faith lesson to show God's hand in each situation. During the past seven years I have emailed these stories weekly to hundreds of friends, family and business associates as my own personal ministry. This book includes some of those stories. I also host a website, www.ChristianFaithStories.com, to make additional stories available.

The best qualificaions any of us have to make a difference for others is a belief that Jesus Christ is our Lord and Savior. I want Him to be part of every aspect of my life. My hope is you will see God at work daily in your life and you will be inspired to share your faith with others. God will give you the tools and strength as you carry out the Great Commission.

Then the eleven disciples went to Galilee, to the mountain where Jesus had told them to go. When they saw him, they worshipped him; but some doubted. Then Jesus came to them and said, "All authority in heaven and on earth has been given to me. Therefore go and make disciples of all nations, baptizing them in the name of the Father and of the Son and of the Holy Spirit, and teaching them to obey everything I have commanded you. And surely I am with you always, to the very end of the age" (Matthew 28:16-20 NIV).

CPSIA information can be obtained at www.ICGtesting.com
Printed in the USA
BVOW07s2129090315

390854BV00001B/2/P